TEN

TEN Words!

Reflections from the Ten Commandments.

S. Robert Maddox

TEN

Published by Redefining Faith Resources

Scripture quotations are from The Holy Bible, English Standard Version® (ESV®), copyright © 2001 by Crossway, a publishing ministry of Good News Publishers. Used by permission. All rights reserved.

Copyright © 2015 by S. Robert Maddox

No portion of this publication may be reproduced, stored in a retrieval system or transmitted in any form by any means - except for brief quotations in published reviews - without the prior written permission of the author.

ISBN: 978-0-9903912-1-0

DEDICATION

To those searching for trustworthy guidelines that build caring and respectful relationships with children, career, church, and community.

CONTENTS

Foreword	Larry Griswold	1
Prologue	Recognition	5
Introduction	One and Zero	7
1st Word	Covenant	11
2nd Word	Loyalty	23
3rd Word	Esteem	33
4th Word	Remember	43
5th Word	Honor	55
6th Word	Assassination	69
7th Word	Betrayal	81
8th Word	Pilfering	99
9th Word	Falsehood	111
10th Word	Greed	123
Final Word	Love	133
	Acknowledgements	145

About the Author 147

Books by the author 149

FOREWORD

It is a personal honor to be requested to pen a few words of introduction to this latest work of my friend, Bob Maddox. Friends write nice things about friends, so it is not out of the ordinary that friends and close acquaintances would be given such opportunity.

As a friend of long-standing, I would be prone to give Bob's writing a read…because I know him and have journeyed a good portion of life with him. But to all who connect to this book, I am attempting to answer YOUR question, namely "**Why should I read THIS book?**"

This book is **timely**.

In a day in which life's gyroscope and guardrails seem absent, a clear re-visit of God's basic words is merited. What God wrote on physical tablets for

Moses is designed to be written on the "tablets of our hearts." These words will still serve us well, in spite of the warp-speed of change our generations have experienced. These words are moorings for our lives and are much-needed by all people of all persuasions and all generations. This book will refresh familiar truths. Give it a read.

The author is **credible**.

A brief scan of the bio of Bob will let you know, this is not an author who's been sitting in the grandstand…he's been on the playing field of life and ministry. The descriptors of Bob's life and assignments (pastor, teacher, college executive, elder of the church, life-coach, volleyball-coach, father, grandfather), all indicate to the reader "he's been there," and speaks from experience that counts.

Bob Maddox is **authentic**.

It is here that my years of personal connection with the author might mean something to your inquiry – Bob Maddox off-camera is authentic. I have witnessed the private moments of others who somehow "change faces" when the red-camera light goes off. I will attest…Bob Maddox in private and public are one and the same. Such veracity of life will permeate the pages of this book.

My Foreword is complete. Keep reading. Better

words are yet to come.

> Larry H. Griswold
> Plainfield, Illinois

S. ROBERT MADDOX

PROLOGUE

RECOGNITION

These reflections are the outgrowth of reading a book years ago on the Ten Commandments written by Dr. Laura Schlessinger, a syndicated radio personality and dedicated Jew, and Rabbi Stewart Vogel, an Orthodox Jew. The meditations were influenced by their approach and absorb some of their observations. If you happen to come across a copy of their work in a library or used bookstore I highly recommend you borrow, or purchase, and give it a read.

This work attempts to provide, as a New Testament follower of Jesus, personal thoughts and a fresh treatment of the older covenant directives, especially to those in a faith relationship with God through his Son.

S. ROBERT MADDOX

INTRODUCTION

ONE AND ZERO

While attending college, I worked at the computer center of a national bank in Seattle, Washington, having over 70 regional banking locations. Initially, the operation was part of a local branch in the university district of the city.

Wanting to purchase the most up-to-date computer, the bank constructed a new complex in Tukwila, near the Southgate Mall and Sea-Tac Airport. The facility covered an entire city block. Half of the building accommodated the numerous computer components, each piece considerably large.

I learned the computer language COBOL (Common Business-Oriented Language) and knew how to create operations using a keypunch machine.

Large stacks of cards were necessary for designing the simplest applications. Today, I sit at a desk using a laptop with more capabilities than a computer that covered half a city block.

Computer science became possible by using the two integers *one* and *zero*. Combining these numbers in a variety of configurations has made personal electronic devices a mainstay of connectedness throughout the world. *One* and *zero* have greatly influenced everyday decisions and altered fundamental actions.

IBM produced a documentary in 1977 showing an imaginary trip through outer and inner space. Using 40 *Powers of Ten,* viewers journeyed from the greatest galaxies to the smallest microcosms of the human body. *Ten* has proven to be the window to unending discoveries.

Numbers have also proven to hold special significance in Scripture. Biblical numerology is the study of recurring numbers and gives attention to possible meanings, both literal and symbolic. Having led some people to mystical extremes, theologians are cautious assigning too much significance to numbers. The following are a few that seemingly create symbolic patterns in Scripture:

One—unity and absolute singleness; the Lord is one.

Three—divine perfection and holiness; God is a Holy Trinity.

Four—the pillars of the Temple; the types of soil in the Parable.

Six—the first human couple was created on the sixth day. The antichrist is referred to with three sixes, the perfect representative of rebellious and arrogant mankind.

Seven—completeness. Creation was completed in seven days. The number is especially significant in the writings of John, completing the picture of Jesus in his gospel narrative and finishing the revelation of him at the end of time.

Eight—victory. Eight survived the flood; circumcision was performed on the eighth day.

Nine—abundance. Nine character attributes are expressed in the Spirit fruit; nine grace actions are manifested in the Spirit gift.

Ten—testimonies. Governing guidelines and the tithe (demonstrating respect with 10%).

Twelve—divine authority and sovereignty. Twelve foundations and twelve gates are part of the New Jerusalem.

Thirty—sorrow. Moses' death was mourned for

thirty days; Jesus was betrayed for thirty pieces of silver.

Forty—testing and trial. Forty days of flooding, forty years of wandering, and forty days of temptation.

Fifty—liberty and jubilee. The Holy Spirit came fifty days after the resurrection of Jesus.

Seventy—justice. Seventy elders of Israel helped establish and administer rules. The nation spent seventy years in captivity as judgment for disobedience.

The numbers *one* and *zero* not only play a role in advancing computers, mathematics, and science but also a lifestyle. Designed into the social fiber of humanity are TEN Words, inspired guidelines for gaining purpose and fulfillment. The integers *one* and *zero* merge, defining and giving expression to divine love and devotion.

This book is a compilation of meditations about the roadmap to a stable and satisfying life. Hopefully, every chapter will provide clarity as well as application, helping you successfully navigate each day with contentment. You were designed to enjoy all aspects of living through *the strength of TEN*.

FIRST WORD

COVENANT

And God spoke all these words, saying, "I am the LORD your God, who brought you out of the land of Egypt, out of the house of slavery. "You shall have no other gods before me. "You shall not make for yourself a carved image, or any likeness of anything that is in heaven above, or that is in the earth beneath, or that is in the water under the earth. You shall not bow down to them or serve them, for I the LORD your God am a jealous God, visiting the iniquity of the fathers on the children to the third and the fourth generation of those who hate me, but showing steadfast love to thousands of those who love me and keep my commandments. "You shall not take the name of the LORD your God in vain, for the LORD will not hold him guiltless who takes his name in vain. "Remember the Sabbath day, to keep it holy.

Six days you shall labor, and do all your work, but the seventh day is a Sabbath to the LORD your God. On it you shall not do any work, you, or your son, or your daughter, your male servant, or your female servant, or your livestock, or the sojourner who is within your gates. For in six days the LORD made heaven and earth, the sea, and all that is in them, and rested on the seventh day. Therefore the LORD blessed the Sabbath day and made it holy. "Honor your father and your mother, that your days may be long in the land that the LORD your God is giving you. "You shall not murder. "You shall not commit adultery. "You shall not steal. "You shall not bear false witness against your neighbor. "You shall not covet your neighbor's house; you shall not covet your neighbor's wife, or his male servant, or his female servant, or his ox, or his donkey, or anything that is your neighbor's." (Exodus 20:1-17)

The Ten Commandments has served as moral directives for centuries. Many learn a simplified version as children. Teenagers and adults could benefit by exploring them in a more developed reading.

The rules of law in America were initially based on this ethical compass, designed to bring people individually and corporately into peace and tranquility. Judges, however, are discouraged from displaying these so-called *inflammatory* ideas on courtroom walls, supposedly infringing upon an irrational separation of church and state. By attempting to compartmentalize life between *sacred* and *secular*, thoughts and emotions are increasingly maladjusted.

The US House of Representatives entertained legislation to display the Ten Commandments in public schools. The debate centered on which version would be exhibited—Liturgical, Protestant, or Jewish? Unable to agree upon a universally accepted rendering, the action was deemed not feasible.

The only place anyone can learn these ten ethical boundaries is in a religious community.

Why?

Why should anyone know the Ten Commandments? A universal standard of morality is required for humanity to survive intact. Standards should never be geared toward temporal things—popular concepts, majority opinions, or social trends; all of which are fleeting. Ethics are best built upon ageless truths, preferably designed by God, tested and proven beneficial to everyone's betterment.

Values develop a conscience, which dictates behavior. Conduct determines the excellence of life and the significance of someone's participation in the lives of others. But what are correct values, what will give significance to personal actions?

Answering these questions starts by examining, *"I am the Lord your God, who brought you out of Egypt, out of the land of slavery."* (Exodus 20:1)

Words!

The title *Ten Commandments* comes from Deuteronomy. "And he declared to you his covenant, which he commanded you to perform, that is, the Ten Commandments, and he wrote them on two tablets of stone." (Deuteronomy 4:13) A Jewish Bible my wife regularly reads translates the heading as *Ten Words*—pronouncements, instead of directives, about right living. The interpretation is important when looking at the First Word.

Some religious groups add to the first statement, "You shall have no other gods before me," (V.3) making the declaration a prohibition against serving multiple gods and directing people to have an exclusive relationship with the one True God. Other faiths incorporate the phrase into the next proclamation that addresses idolatry. Without the phrase, the First Word lacks a sense of command.

The first of the TEN Words does not promote belief in a single God but states his absolute rule: "I am *the* Lord…", indicating he has the divine right to provide and initiate a course of action for living.

Without acknowledging his authority to reign over life, the remaining statements simply become *suggestions*, open to personal discretion. Without pronouncing God exists in an elevated position over all living things, a person can reason, "I will follow these guidelines if I feel like it, personally think they are a good idea, or consider them not too troublesome." Without stating status, the decrees are drained of a sense of duty.

He is the universal Lord, whether a person has special standings with him or not. Someone without faith in God cannot negate his right to make directives impacting everyone.

Questions about influence.

Who can adequately define pure virtue and polluted vice? Only God can decide a morality reflective of his perfect nature.

Where do most people presently base a standard of living; if God is not in charge, then who is? The only alternative is for everyone to be their own ruling force. The focus becomes self-determination, self-expression, and self-fulfillment, concepts very much in vogue today and heavily promoted in schools and universities.

To some degree, self-expression is good but must be evaluated as either right or wrong. Some selfishly consider adult sexual activity with small children acceptable. Some also uncaringly think eliminating the weak, ill, or different is okay.

Is a self-focused perspective always fair and good for the whole? Not according to the teachings of Jesus. He taught life is more fulfilling when thinking of others over personal wants and wishes.

Can people not believing in God be moral? Anyone can draft a structure deemed proper, but usually they give attention to culturally accepted norms, or the edicts of a ruling class, or the legislative action of the majority, or personal preference, or individual urges, or what the immediate situation dictates, or what seems expedient. Concepts and opinions are largely subjective, which is often toxic and even lethal.

What person is capable of perfectly determining, without prejudice, what is right? No one! Ultimately the decision of what is right and wrong must come from an outside source. Individual assessments, observations, and logic do not fully provide a framework for a universally honorable way of life.

TEN

What is a major difference between people establishing good standards and God creating them? When people come up with rules, they are normally motivated by, "What's right for me?" When living by divine principles, the focus is, "What's best for everyone?" His guidelines are an upright and universal way of promoting fairness that enrich the welfare of one and all.

What has become God's assignment in life for most people? Having little or no personal obligation to connect, God is simply a comforter. Without any sense of devotion, he is someone people go to for support, a resource in times of pain or during challenges. Any commitment to the Lord is only as deemed necessary for vital and critical relief. Any form of dedication is relegated to the realm of individual preference.

The requirement!

The First Word gives special attention to entering a heartfelt relationship with God, stating, "I am the Lord *your* God…", something comparable to vows in a wedding covenant.

Marriage is more than a piece of paper, or a verbal commitment at a ceremony; it is consecrated. Personal preference is demoted to a secondary role in the marital union; there are hallowed duties and obligations. Love is a *verb* more than a *noun*, an action more than a state of mind.

A consecrated relationship with God can also be compared to a parent and child connection, the outgrowth of marriage.

Parental rules often seem to children as a nuisance—restrictive and random. A parent tries to explain but if this does not work the matter is resolved by simply saying, "These guidelines are binding because I am the parent and you are the child. I brought you into the world, feed you, clothe you, and shelter you. Therefore, I establish the standards of the home." The statement establishes a unique position of influence.

Parental rules are binding because a parent gives them. The TEN Words are binding because God gave them, the perfect and divine Creator of all creation.

Through the model of husband/wife and parent/child, the covenant made with God is a combination of obligations and benefits. Salvation produces thankfulness and appreciation for the saving grace found in Jesus, and gratitude is expressed by living with a divine standard. A truthful and transparent life becomes the ongoing visible recognition of God's presence.

TEN

Brought out!

The remainder of the guideline reads, "…who brought you out of Egypt, out of the land of slavery." Exodus reveals the cruel living conditions of Israel in Egypt. The story accurately depicts a world seemingly giving safety and security but eventually showing itself for what it really is, a place of bondage, oppression, misery, and pain.

Attached to a divine covenant relationship are deliverance and freedom. His ways are not restrictive but just the opposite, they are liberating. By making Jesus *your* Lord, he alone sets you free from a world falsely portrayed as peaceful and safe, and ushers you into an everlasting life.

The First Word is an acknowledgment of the God who has a solemn right over your life. Involvement with him through a relationship with his Son brings freedom. Behavior becomes impacted as in marriage and, like a child, you can question the guidelines, but the ultimate answer is a just, pure, perfect, and non-biased Heavenly Father knows what is best.

Your move!

There was an officer in the Navy who had always dreamed of commanding a battleship. He finally achieved the dream and was given the newest and proudest vessel in the fleet. On a stormy night, as the ship plowed through the seas, the captain was on the bridge and spotted a strange light rapidly closing in.

Immediately, he ordered the radio operator to send a message to the unidentified craft, "Alter your course ten degrees to the south."

Only a moment passed before a reply came, "Alter your course ten degrees to the north."

Determined that his ship would not take a backseat to another, the captain snapped out the command, "By order of the Captain alter your course ten degrees!"

The response came back, "Seaman Third Class Jones is telling you to alter your course ten degrees."

Infuriated, the captain grabbed the microphone and yelled, "Alter your course, I am a battleship."

The reply came, "Alter your course, I am a lighthouse."

No matter how important someone may think they are, the TEN Words stand as an unchanging beacon. All other courses must be altered.

TEN

A simple prayer.

Are you presently in a covenant relationship with the Lord? This has been made possible through the death and resurrection of Jesus. Why not enter into genuine freedom and authentic peace? Talk to God about your situation and allow him to alter your focus and direction. He offers a better way to live.

"God, I recognize your divine standings over my life and want a grace relationship with you. I come to you fully realizing my failures, making it impossible to connect with you by personal merit. I am far from perfect and have nothing to offer except my sincere love and absolute devotion.

"Lord Jesus, thank you for being the substitute for my shortcomings and for presenting my petition for mercy to the Heavenly Father. Heavenly Father, thank you for canceling my eternal debt, caused by pride and rebellion. Holy Spirit, thank you for enabling me to better demonstrate my thankfulness, providing critical help to live according to divinely given guidelines."

S. ROBERT MADDOX

SECOND WORD

LOYALTY

The First Word is more a *statement* than *command*, declaring God exists in a place of absolute rule and can rightfully establish guidelines for everyone. Instead of being prohibitive, the directive is about entering a meaningful relationship with the Lord. Covenants have benefits and obligations. The *benefit* is deliverance and freedom from bondage, oppression, misery, and pain. God can set a person free from a world falsely portrayed as peaceful and safe. The *obligations* are expressed in the other nine pronouncements.

The TEN Words are not exclusively communicated in Exodus and Deuteronomy. All of scripture confirms the pitfalls of ignoring these instructions. Additional Bible passages associated with each guideline is included in the following chapters.

Now while Paul was waiting for them at Athens, his spirit was provoked within him as he saw that the city was full of idols…. So Paul, standing in the midst of the Areopagus, said: "Men of Athens, I perceive that in every way you are very religious. For as I passed along and observed the objects of your worship, I found also an altar with this inscription, 'To the unknown god.' What therefore you worship as unknown, this I proclaim to you." (Acts 17:16, 22-23)

The city of Athens was a city glutted with gods. They were the world's foremost collector of deities, having ransacked the theologies of many civilizations and gathering every idol they could possibly transport by cart and ship. Figurines lined both sides of many roadways and covered a rocky hillside called Areopagus. Later, the Parthenon would be built at this site.

The story surrounding the *unknown god* goes back to a time when the city was experiencing a plague. They regularly worshiped and sacrificed to numerous idols, but the scourge continued. Out of desperation, a delegation was sent to the island of Crete to fetch a man named Epimenides. He told them the god they angered was unknown to them and gave the plan to invoke his help. The proposal included acknowledging ignorance of the god's name.

The strategy seemed to work. They wanted to dedicate an altar, but to whom? Rather than offend this god seemingly pleased with their admission of ignorance, they named the altar, "To an unknown god."

By the time the Apostle Paul came to the city, a couple hundred more icons had been added. Idolatry, by its very nature, has a built-in inflation factor. Once people reject the one True God in favor of lesser deities, they eventually discover it takes an infinite number of gods to fill his place. Paul saw Athens prostituting the sacred privilege of worship upon mere wood and stone and his soul became troubled.

Nations today are quickly walking on the same pathway as Athens. Like ancient Greece, cultures enamored with human intelligence and knowledge will bow to anything promising greater wisdom. Inevitably, arrogance, pride, and folly soon follow. The headlines of major news sources reveal many societies are firmly held in the grips of idolatry.

The Second Word prohibits recognizing or creating other gods and making images to worship them. The purpose is to negate all subordinates from causing disloyalty, further estranging people from the one True God.

Describing God

What does the Lord God look like? Children tend to consider him a reflection of their parents. Perceptions about God are influenced more by fathers than mothers; the Lord usually becomes related to the greater authority figure, with their balance of power and love. If mom and dad are loving, fair, strong, firm, devoted, and forgiving, a child sees God in more wholesome ways. If they are abusive, cruel, unbending, angry, and unfaithful, the perception of him is tainted.

Scripture does not focus on describing God's looks. Comments about his hand or face are mentioned, but the form of the hand and look of the face are not described. Instead, attention is given to what he does and says. He is known as *righteous*, not as handsome; he is characterized as *loving*, not as muscular.

What is the difference between the one True God and every lesser god? Other deities are connected to nature and represent various forces. In ancient times, gods were attached to rain, wind, and the sun, either requiring appeasement or sometimes manipulated for personal gain and survival. Idolatry involves attempting to sway events for personal advantage.

God is not an aspect of the natural realm but is greater than the universe. No one should lower their expectations to mere human discernment. People are mortal and limited: ears can only hear specific sound levels; eyes can only see certain sizes of matter and specific kinds of light. To believe the extent of deity is only what is seen, heard, or touched is foolish.

God is greater than form and beyond sensory perception. Being unable to know what he looks like is not evidence against his existence but evidence that he is beyond human comprehension.

Focusing on God's physical nature is idolatrous. Reduced to human description, his true and ultimate power becomes limited and his motives appear frivolous and changeable.

Lesser gods

Idolatry is an effort on the part of people to control circumstances. To justify personal desires and weaknesses, many dangerously create gods. In idolatry, indiscriminate cravings achieve validity, such as cruelty and brutality.

In idolatry, no one must ever rise above

themselves. A society without God, or one in which false deities reign, is a place where injustice ultimately dwells. The millions murdered under godless dictators, leaders of totalitarian regimes, give testimony of the ugliness of self-deity.

Like the idols of Athens, the list of lesser gods is potentially endless. Here are a few prominent controlling forces:

Superstitions are a back-door acknowledgment of other gods or spirits having power over life. Avoiding walking under ladders or throwing spilled salt over the left shoulder represent fear of unidentifiable consequences. When activities are altered on Friday the 13th and anxiety is caused by a broken mirror, superstitious homage is being expressed to mysterious powers.

Some people enjoy starting the day looking at *horoscopes*. What kind of day should be expected? What should be done and what should be avoided? Astrology is another way people escape being responsible for their lives. Allowing forces of nature to dictate actions, based upon zodiac interpretations of stars and the confluence of moons and planets, is directly connected to ancient idolatry. Wholehearted devotion to God is only possible when he is the sole motivator of behavior.

TEN

Society is deeply engrossed with creating false idols of *celebrities*—athletes, actors, musicians, crowned royalty. Many talk like them, wear similar clothes, and buy products endorsed by them. Every available bit of gossip is read about them and, ironically, after being idolized, their downfall is relished. Their failure and disgrace are enjoyed because they suddenly appear no better than anyone. A sense is restored that they are just like everyone else.

Other lesser gods exist but these three, though often treated casually and downplayed jokingly, control thoughts, feelings, moods, attitudes, conversations, and actions.

The top idol

Scriptures reveal a *Holy* Trinity (Father, Son, and Holy Spirit) and an *evil* trinity (devil, antichrist, and false prophet), but the number one idol is the *selfish* trinity (me, myself, and I).

If humans, made in the image and likeness of God, is the ultimate and climactic expression of creation, they are also the object of the highest form of idolatry. Like children who believe the world revolves around them, thinking too much of yourself turns you into an idol. You become your own god with an unhealthy sense of sovereignty, filling the world with selfishness and hypocrisy. The *selfie* generation is losing the ability to see the role God plays in life and he is ending up being nothing but a favorite lucky charm.

Four areas of selfishness are increasingly idolatrous:

The idolatry of human feelings. Feelings have become veritable temples of worship. They have been elevated to unrealistic levels of honor and importance. Much of psychoanalysis is delving into the depths of emotional turmoil.

Many see the agony of victimhood as a throne upon which to worship, and erroneously make this the focal point of their attention. Feeling bad about life, or sensing low self-esteem, or not wishing to do right, or believing no one is nice, does not excuse wrongful behavior.

Human emotions easily become illogical, unhinged, erratic, and bizarre. People often do not know how they feel. Some mistake feelings for moods, which can be the product of poor eating habits, insufficient sleep, or lack of exercise. When the ultimate authority is *feelings* a person bows to self-idolatry.

Many acts of aggression that happen in schools

and public places are caused by an unhealthy elevation of feelings, attackers feeling rejection and wanting retaliation. Doing right is not contingent upon feelings or presence of mind. People are to rise above themselves instead of committing idolatry by raising themselves above what is ethical.

The idolatry of human desires. Idolatry is committed when desires are put ahead of values, responsibilities, and obligations. When people know no law other than their cravings, God is not preeminent in their life.

The idolatry of human looks. Whether the physique of the body or the features of the face, many are obsessed with appearance and enamored with looks. Some are making cosmetic alterations in medical clinics a bloody altar of sacrificial worship. The theater and the arts admire a perfect appearance, much like the finely sculptured nude statues of ancient Greece.

The idolatry of human ideas. When people hold any idea or activity higher than God, even a pious deed wrongly pursued is idolatry. Some use religion to elevate themselves and magnify personal attention. God ends up reduced to a personal attendant, serving wants and weaknesses. Religion can become its own endpoint. The Second Word frustrates those looking to religion for achievement, promotion, and control—looking to faith to accomplish questionable pursuits.

Faith in God is about him. When he becomes your focal point, his desire becomes your ambition, his method becomes your mission, then life is holy and complete. God is the center of faith and only his blessing brings purpose.

The Second Word

"You shall have no other gods before me. You shall not make for yourself a carved image, or any likeness of anything that is in heaven above, or that is in the earth beneath, or that is in the water under the earth. You shall not bow down to them or serve them, for I the LORD your God am a jealous God, visiting the iniquity of the fathers on the children to the third and the fourth generation of those who hate me, but showing steadfast love to thousands of those who love me and keep my commandments." (Exodus 20:3-6)

The Apostle John demonstrated a lifetime of proven ministry and ended a letter giving a significant warning for today: "Beloved, keep yourselves from idols." (1 John 5:21)

Great advice! Apply it to your life.

THIRD WORD

ESTEEM

The First Word declares God can legitimately establish guidelines for everyone. People are invited into a covenant union with him and gain freedom from bondage and oppression.

The Second Word prohibits recognizing the gods of others and making images to worship them. People are to negate all subordinates that diminish godliness and further estrange them from the one True God.

The Third Word is seen in an incident recorded in the book of Acts: *Then some of the itinerant Jewish exorcists undertook to invoke the name of the Lord Jesus over those who had evil spirits, saying, "I adjure you by the Jesus whom Paul proclaims."*

Seven sons of a Jewish high priest named Sceva were doing this. But the evil spirit answered them, "Jesus I know, and Paul I recognize, but who are you?" And the man in whom was the evil spirit leaped on them, mastered all of them and overpowered them, so that they fled out of that house naked and wounded. And this became known to all the residents of Ephesus, both Jews and Greeks. And fear fell upon them all, and the name of the Lord Jesus was extolled. (Acts 19:13-17)

Moses wrote, *"You shall not take the name of the LORD your God in vain, for the LORD will not hold him guiltless who takes his name in vain."* (Exodus 20:7) Anytime the name of the Lord is misused, the result is a hollow and futile portrayal of him.

Names identify

Names identify and define. Selecting the name of a child is significant. People often take on various characteristics of their name.

My wife and I carefully considered what to call our four children: Nikole (spelled the Hawaiian way) is Greek for *victory*; Nannette is Hebrew for *grace*; Zachary is Hebrew for *remembered by the Lord*; and, Stephen is Greek for *crown*. All our children have taken on noble qualities.

TEN

My name is associated with my father. Although not regularly used by me, *Stanley* means *dweller at a rocky meadow, sturdiness*, implying that rocky moments need someone with a durable and steadfast spirit for survival. The middle name *Robert* means *shining with fame*, suggesting motivated by excellence.

Names in scripture often recall the circumstances of birth, reflect character, or depict destiny. God changed the name Abram to Abraham in preparation for fulfilling his future. Sarai, his wife, was changed to Sarah, giving her a new standing before others. Jacob, his grandson, was given the name Israel in response to an all-night tug-a-war with the Lord.

In the twentieth century, during the unsettling 60's, people changed names as a means of defiance, identifying themselves with plants and animals, planets and stars.

God takes the issue of names and naming seriously. The Third Word has an immediate threat of punishment: "The Lord will not hold anyone guiltless who misuses His name." The good standing and honor of the Lord are to be protected.

Why is vainly using his name an issue? He is a God of relationships. An association with him must give the clearest definition of holiness to others. A corrupt name diminishes a clear belief and accurate awe for him. When a person enters an abiding union with God through his son Jesus, attitudes and actions should not defame his righteous character and compassionate actions.

Names describe

The names of God in scripture represent how he reveals himself.

The Lord appeared to an elderly Abram as "El Shaddai"—God Almighty. *Shaddai* is derived from an ancient language of the Middle East and refers to mountains or open spaces, indicating vastness and greatness. The term speaks of power to control and to limit, a description of majesty and magnificence.

Moses was told at a burning-bush encounter the name, "I AM." No matter how impossible a situation appears, God is actively present. When delivering Israel from Egypt, the always current God promised to be with them. He is continually near those with unwavering faith.

The Hebrew letters translated into YHWH (often pronounced *Yahweh*) means *Lord God*. The name was so sacred that it was forbidden to be recited except on Yom Kippur by the High Priest within the

TEN

Holy of Holies—the holiest day, by the holiest person, in the holiest place. Out of regard for its great sanctity, his name was *Adonai* the rest of the year, during prayer and scripture reading.

Having various names reveals the Lord is not limited; the one True God is beyond a person's narrow perception. Ancient gods had specific names, usually expressing a partial sphere of authority and control. By invoking the name of these gods, people attempted to maneuver and accomplish their personal preference.

The possession of a name implies influence. The first man Adam was assigned to name all the animals, symbolizing dominance. People in times past considered names powerful, providing greater authority.

The one True God, however, is different from all other gods. His name is used in blessing, not for selfish favors. People are unable to trick him into performing their will when invoking his name.

This was the issue described in Acts 19. Seven itinerant exorcists, for a fee, claimed they could cast out evil spirits by using a *mysterious* name. Success in casting out demons was not implied, only the attempt. They made a ritual using the name of Jesus and failed. *Ritual* never fools evil. Only the *reality* of

Jesus, as manifested by the Holy Spirit, causes demons to flee.

The importance of esteem

God's name is often misused. A failure to show proper esteem diminishes his standings.

Irreverence is displayed toward God by using his name frivolously. Years ago, a television commercial suggested God was unable to get a large quantity of brochures printed on time, but a certain printing company could. His name was used playfully to gain customers. The nature of God was trivialized.

Adding worth to a product by suggesting God's endorsement is also inappropriate. Although appearing cute or humorous, his name ends up flippantly used.

V*ulgarity*, even without invoking his name, does not show proper esteem to God or respect to those created in his image and likeness. Crudely referencing parts of the body modestly covered or using the "S-word" and "F-bomb" is never acceptable. Offensive comments and gestures diminish the light within and are not an emulation of Jesus, the light of the world.

TEN

What are people doing when obscenely invoking God's name? They are displaying anger at frustration, failure, or misfortune. Or, they are attacking God for something they do not understand. Or, they are blaming God for actions and the consequences that follow. In other words, people misuse the name of God by accusing him of being something less than he is and having only human attributes.

While attending High School, a classmate became angry and used several cuss words. A friend sitting near me quietly murmured, "He who swears has a limited vocabulary."

Occasionally, I teach at a high school and can attest many students still have a limited vocabulary. Using foul language broadcasts ignorance.

Failing to live honorably makes the Lord look bad. Many people falter under the power of peer pressure, the longing for popularity, or a fear of rejection. Should blending in be the basis of behavior?

What actions should others see in Christ followers? What questionable activities should be avoided? Is a diminishing of his presence worth the price of gaining acceptance?

Anytime someone acts badly, they shame the name of God. Even conduct without evil intentions (coming from apathy or laziness) has the power to profane. Every time faith and beliefs are brought into disrepute, his name is desecrated.

Claiming God said something when he did not is a misuse of his name, which frequently happens in religious settings. When unwise actions become questioned by others, some respond, "The Lord told me to do it." In a split second, the fault was no longer a poor personal decision but supposedly authored by God. A higher authority was invoked to sanction questionable conduct.

The Third Word comes with an *immediate* threat of punishment. If someone chooses to say, "The Lord told me" when God has not spoken, they should give warning, so people can get out of the way before lightning strikes.

Making an oath and not following through is a misuse of his name. Pledges and vows are important to the one who makes promises and keeps oaths. God makes commitments and, to demonstrate the truthfulness of his words, seals them with various signs, such as the shadow going back ten steps for Hezekiah. (2 Kings 20:1-11) People cannot invoke any name higher than God when obligating themselves. Failing to keep a promise dishonors the name of an oath-keeping God.

Insincere confession and repentance are a vain use of his name. The expression "I am sorry" is misused worldwide. Genuine sorrow heals but insincere apologies cause further damage. What is motivating the stated remorse: disappointment for poor behavior or simply attempting to avoid consequences?

Genuine sorrow promises *not* to repeat the offense. Regret alone is rarely sufficient. Sincere repentance expresses grief over previous conduct and a commitment to not walk the same pathway again.

Esteem is violated when cursing God, profaning his name, misrepresenting him, pretending a special relationship with him for personal gain, using his name to manipulate, invoking his name while engaged in wayward acts, and when making promises with no intention to honor.

Reverence

Everyone should enter into a personal relationship with the Lord, reject the false authority of all other gods, and give esteem to the sacred nature of this divine association.

Language reflects who you are and conveys what you want. God gave the gift of reason and communication, something not bestowed on lesser creatures. The ability to clearly verbalize thoughts should be appreciated and used with reverence and caution.

The care a follower of Jesus takes to not misrepresent the Lord is a sign of love. Every time his standings are stained, there is a risk of rift from the one True God. Uphold his good name and protect his honor. Show esteem!

FOURTH WORD

REMEMBER

"If you turn back your foot from the Sabbath, from doing your pleasure on my holy day, and call the Sabbath a delight and the holy day of the LORD honorable; if you honor it, not going your own ways, or seeking your own pleasure, or talking idly; then you shall take delight in the LORD, and I will make you ride on the heights of the earth; I will feed you with the heritage of Jacob your father, for the mouth of the LORD has spoken." (Isaiah 58:13-14)

Isaiah was a seer and spokesman for God in Jerusalem, prophesying during the threatening expansion of the Assyrian empire. He lived during the reign of four Judean kings, beginning with Uzziah and ending with Hezekiah—a period of approximately fifty years.

In the true spirit of a prophet, there was forth-telling (truth for today) and foretelling (truth about tomorrow). He spoke about national sins leading to divine judgment and gave hope for a day of restoration. The first part of the book highlights *judgment* and the second *salvation*.

In the second portion, emphasizing redemption from rebellion, one day each week is considered special to the Lord. Isaiah declares divine joy and the ability to live on top of everyday challenges are connected to honoring a Rest Day.

The First Word states God is in a place of authority and you should have a love relationship with him. The Second directs you to reject the authority of all other gods, especially the triune god of me, myself, and I. The Third emphasizes esteeming the good name of God and protecting his honor.

The Fourth Word declares, *"Remember the Sabbath day, to keep it holy. Six days you shall labor, and do all your work, but the seventh day is a Sabbath to the LORD your God. On it you shall not do any work, you, or your son, or your daughter, your male servant, or your female servant, or your livestock, or the sojourner who is within your gates. For in six days the LORD made heaven and earth, the sea, and all that is in them, and rested on the seventh day. Therefore the LORD blessed the Sabbath day and made it holy."* (Exodus 20:8-11)

Time

The issue of time is huge, the hottest commodity today. Money can often be replaced, but not time. The attributes of success are less about owning expensive items and more about having time for pleasures and other pursuits. Success is having a schedule that allows for family, worthwhile causes, and leisure.

The crisis of time is growing increasingly serious. Discretionary time is declining. Time for house upkeep, car maintenance, laundry, relaxation, volunteering, and church involvement is quickly evaporating. Some decline is real and others are perceived.

A decline in time is *real* by people working massive hours, some having multiple jobs and experiencing long commutes to and from the workplace on congested roadways. The decline is *real* by personal electronic devices increasing the pace of work rather than diminishing it. The decline is *real* by parents spending more time rushing children from one activity to another instead of establishing restrictions.

A decline in time is *perceived* by expecting an instant response to everything. When something does not quickly happen, people feel *pressed for time*. Convenience has lent itself to making people feel more rushed.

To the issues surrounding time, God instituted a day each week for reflection.

Rest

Understanding the guideline involves the activities of creation. Genesis states God created the first man and woman on the sixth day; what follows is rest.

"And on the seventh day God finished his work that he had done, and he rested on the seventh day from all his work that he had done. So God blessed the seventh day and made it holy, because on it God rested from all his work that he had done in creation." (Genesis 2:2-3)

The first six days gives attention to perfect craftsmanship and the highest possible workmanship, yet the seventh is the *only* day considered consecrated. The first six days God considered *good*; the seventh He made *holy*. The creation of physical things ceased, and spirituality was established the next day. God proclaimed time holy and holiness ageless.

The first six days of creation provided a world without purpose; the seventh gave meaning to all that took place. Creation is about a planet designed to express worship to God.

The seventh day is not just a segment of creation in which nothing happened. Instead, God gave his blessing and sanctified time. More than an opportunity for recreation, the day representing one-seventh of the week allows a person to go beyond the focus of everyday existence and remember the meaning of life.

The Rest Day is ordained for spirituality but only a person's actions can bring the potential to reality. The day set apart by God reminds people that the ultimate meaning of life is found in him, and life needs to be regularly consecrated the way he sanctified the completion of creation.

Devout Jews honor Saturday and Christ-followers regard Sunday special. Both days commemorate his redemptive act, God bringing people back to their intended purpose.

Jews memorialize redemption as seen in the exodus from Egypt. The dividing of the Red Sea is *the* miracle of the Old Testament.

Followers of Jesus celebrate redemption on the first day of the week, the morning when Christ came from the grave—the Lord's Day. His resurrection is *the* miracle of the New Testament.

Complete deliverance and freedom from sin are honored one day every week. Biblical rest means regularly dedicating time to worship and to intensifying a relationship with the Lord. Life changes from ordinary to blessed.

Not just time off but hallowed

A day has been established each week for unrushed activity. On this day, people are divinely designed to restfully reflect on God and things that pertain to him. Failing to worship has more to do with *excuses* than *reasons* and is often a cover-up for laziness and indifference.

Life will always be full of endless expectations and entertainments, excitements and enticements. People can easily lose sight of what makes living important. For one day everyone is to have freedom from the tyranny of time and break away from the chains of enslavement. For one day there is freedom to pursue the true purpose of life—living for God. Time is given to find *meaning in the moment* and *taking pleasure in his presence*.

TEN

Having to stop and rest is not just about recovering from exhaustion, caused by a week of hard work. Rest is about standing back and viewing life from an eternal perspective. Most people are so busy that they lose sight of life itself. Rest means putting aside common actions and thoughts in order to unwind and appreciate living, about resetting the spiritual clock and becoming reconnected with the ultimate purpose of life. People are to remember weekly that they are dispensable to *business* but not to *God*.

Some rationalize a day spent doing *recreation* fulfills the spirit of the law; they think the day is *re-creating* them. Sports fans and athletics do pray at games, yet asking God to help a team win is questionable. Prayer should lead to matters of eternal value.

Most people require a specific motivation or benefit before participating in an activity. If "What personal advantage will I gain?" is not sufficiently answered, they usually avoid involvement. For many, the idea of pursuing holiness does not seem practical or immediately gratifying. In reality, holiness and a day engaging the Holy One gives tremendous physical as well as spiritual benefits.

The perfect day

First, *quit the rush and get out of the daily grind*. As people grow older, the length of a year seems to decrease until time passes with the blink of an eye. Aging is like a downhill bike ride—speed increases and applying the brakes becomes more difficult. A Rest Day is a carefully placed *stop sign*, bringing a chaotic schedule to a halt. Time passes a little bit slower, so it can be appreciated.

Secondly, *a day for faith, family, and followers of Jesus*! As important as private moments with the Lord, time with others for encouragement, accountability, and correction is equally essential.

The weekly Rest Day is a day given to *faith*, time given to God and to spiritual formation without normal everyday distractions. Why not even use part of the afternoon for literal rest, getting caught up on some deprived sleep, which helps clear up perceptions about grace-living?

Becoming regularly reconnected with *family* members is also important. Meals together become special times for relating to one another and creating meaningful memories.

Spiritually in-tuned parents want the family to believe in God, but eternal development requires dedication, duty, and devotion to spiritual growth. When mom and dad are not working, and children are not engaged in other pursuits, the family can share important aspects of togetherness.

Coming together with other *followers of Jesus* reminds you to abide by the values of the group. You are reminded to consider the well-being of others and not be preoccupied with yourself. In church, you cannot be a private island.

The average week is often too hectic for considering issues about life. People become caught up thinking about schedules and dealing with problems. Gathering to worship and sitting around a supper table when no one must run off to an activity becomes a meaningful moment of thinking about spiritual matters and talking with one another.

One day a week is devoted to not planning or doing every day and routine activities. Maddening thoughts and trivial irritations are given up, the focus becomes thankfulness, appreciation, and gratitude.

The *why* question

My teen years were spent in the 1960's. The youth were rebellious and expressed their defiance in several ways—hair, dress, music, drugs, morality. Various questions troubled them and, left unanswered, prompted poor behavior.

Normally, younger people, while looking at their future, give serious thought to various *how* questions: how do I become successful; how do I fill my place in society; how do I achieve happiness; how do I discover God's will for my life?

The 60's generation wanted *why* questions answered first: why do I exist; why are young people being sent to Vietnam and dying; why do we pursue jobs, get married, buy houses, and build careers?

Not receiving satisfactory answers, my generation opposed the "establishment"—they turned away from the prescribed ways of doing things. When *why* questions are not answered, *how* questions are meaningless.

Each week you need to answer the ultimate why question: why do I live? To worship God! Life makes sense only by regularly resting and remembering your purpose and destiny. The answer keeps all the how questions in balance.

Busy

The first six days of creation were very busy; the last action was mankind coming to life. The seventh day was the first full day Adam and Eve experienced living, the first time this couple went to sleep and woke up discovering another day. They learned life goes on and the purpose of life is directly associated with resting in the Lord.

Every Rest Day, like the first one, should awaken you to a deep awareness of what it means to really live. The day becomes a *this* world sample of the *next* world, providing an opportunity to achieve further holiness in the way you speak and behave.

If you are like most people you are very busy. Busy is good! God was hard at work for six days, considered good when they ended. The question is: will you put aside busyness to experience the blessing of holiness?

A good number of people are frustrated, feeling hopeless, and lacking joy. Are they refusing to stop and reflect on the purpose of life? Six days each week everyone must deal with *how* questions but on the seventh, by focusing on the definitive *why* question, there comes a fresh infusion of divine joy and eternal bliss.

S. ROBERT MADDOX

FIFTH WORD

HONOR

"Honor your father and mother" (this is the first commandment with a promise), "that it may go well with you and that you may live long in the land." (Ephesians 6:2-3)

Jesus answered them, "And why do you break the commandment of God for the sake of your tradition? For God commanded, 'Honor your father and your mother,' and, 'Whoever reviles father or mother must surely die.' But you say, 'If anyone tells his father or his mother, "What you would have gained from me is given to God," he need not honor his father.' So for the sake of your tradition you have made void the word of God. You hypocrites!" (Matthew 15:3-7)

The First Word reveals God is in a place of

authority and wants you to experience freedom from worldly bondage by entering into a covenant with him.

The Second Word rejects the authority of all other gods, even demonic ones: "Therefore, my beloved, flee from idolatry…. What do I imply then? That food offered to idols is anything, or that an idol is anything? No, I imply that what pagans sacrifice they offer to demons and not to God. I do not want you to be participants with demons." (1 Corinthians 10:14, 19-20)

The Third Word emphasizes esteeming God. Every form of communication and activity associated with his name is to be honorable and his supreme standing must be upheld.

The Fourth Word gives attention to remembering. One day each week is designed to reset your inward clock. Six days are spent dealing with *how* questions but the seventh reminds you the reason *why*, restoring balance to everything.

The first six days of creation were declared *good*; the seventh was made *holy*. By sanctifying the day, time is blessed, and holiness is ageless.

How valuable is time?

TEN

To realize the value of ONE YEAR
Ask a student who has failed a grade in school.

To realize the value of ONE MONTH
Ask a mother who has given birth to a premature baby.

To realize the value of ONE WEEK
Ask an editor of a weekly newspaper.

To realize the value of ONE DAY
Ask a person who was born on February 29th.

To realize the value of ONE HOUR
Ask the bride who is waiting to see her groom.

To realize the value of ONE MINUTE
Ask a person who has missed the bus, train, or plane.

To realize the value of ONE SECOND
Ask a person who has avoided an accident.

To realize the value of ONE MILLISECOND
Ask the person who won a silver medal in the Olympics. (Author Unknown)

The Lord wants to add value to your life and time dedicated to him makes this possible. Each week should include occasions given to faith, family, and followers of Jesus.

The Fifth Word reads, *"Honor your father and your mother, that your days may be long in the land that the LORD your God is giving you."* (Exodus 20:12)

Parents

Parenting is not easy. The four children God gave my wife and I have been an education. Our four "in-law" children have added to our knowledge. All are uniquely different.

Our home had foundational rules yet, because of different personalities, they were individually enforced. To one child a stern look was sufficient to produce behavior modification, while to another, in a similar situation, a controlled swat on the rump was required for effectual change. We endeavored to help them build strengths and manage weaknesses. We sought to shape their giftedness while appreciating the abilities of the other siblings.

Only eternity will tell if we were successful. Regardless of how solid or poor our parenting skills, honor is *mandatory*.

TEN

Parental role

The Fifth Word sits in the middle of the TEN Words, serving as a transition. The first four relate to God, the last five relate to those created in his image. Wedged in between is the parent, creating the bridge to all relations. How a child understands relationships, connecting with God and others, is dependent to a large degree on mom and dad. They sit at the crossroads.

The impression of God is shaped by the first *authority figures* in life. Were parents fair and firm, loving and just, compassionate and faithful? Or were they cruel and angry, demanding and selfish, abusive and unbending? They create the platform by which a child sees and understands God.

Parents also decide how children relate to people. An increasing number of moms and dads are making life revolve around their children. Everything is for them. Tragic!

Since the home orbits around the child, he or she believes the world should also (which it will not do), as well as the church (which it must not do). Many kids believe the sun rises and sets on them and have become obnoxious and difficult. And they wonder why no one wants to spend time with them?

The late President John Kennedy attempted to confront this unhealthy mindset with the infamous and inspiring comment: "Ask not what your country can do for you, but what you can do for your country."

Some parents treat their children like superstars, protecting them from consequences for poor behavior. My oldest son as a high school math teacher and his wife as a kindergarten teacher corrected misbehaving students only to experience parental confrontations about their *perfect* child. Like older people, young children (sometimes referred to as innocent) possess rebellious natures and are not helped if left undisciplined.

Are parents protecting a child from punishment to avoid looking or feeling bad about the disaster they have made? Moms and dads easily slip into seeing their children as an extension of themselves and defend them against any attack on their *selfish*-esteem.

Children need parents to show them how to successfully live in society. They are depending on parents to *demand* excellence in behavior.

Parental responsibility

Parents are responsible for teaching ethical

boundaries, which requires time, something many prefer not to give. Several wish to focus on personal wants and wishes and neglect fashioning good values and virtuous conduct in the home. The child ends up not able to do what is right in a culture demanding otherwise.

If parents fail to train, society is forced to correct. No one desires to visit their child in a jail or mental hospital, yet these, as well as the morgue, become tragic alternatives to neglected guidance.

Parents are also responsible for shaping and molding manners, which starts by acting politely and shunning phoniness. Children cannot *learn* selfless qualities until *seeing* kindhearted conduct. Mom and dad set the example.

Teaching manners requires zero tolerance for insolence. Too many kids bad-mouth parents, even in public places. They must be corrected no matter the embarrassment.

Some parents try to be a *buddy* (a very close friend) and neglect to teach. Children can make friends with anyone, only a mom and dad can parent. Abdicating the responsibility to teach children ethics and etiquette cripples them from experiencing success.

Parental reward

The reward of parenting is receiving honor from the family. The words *honor* and *esteem* are sometimes used synonymously but should be treated differently.

The directive is not about esteem, holding mom and dad in the highest regard. Some parents disqualify themselves by poor actions. They have done little to warrant admiration, especially abusive parents. Conduct, however, is not attached to this obligation.

The directive is not about pleasant feelings. Various conflicts are experienced in the dynamics of effective parenting. Sometimes parents and children come out of the turbulent teen years with strong ties—at other times, they hardly escape with any relationship at all. Parents risk *hatred* multiple times and jeopardize losing affection in order to do *what is best*.

The directive is about honor. Children are to behave in a certain way toward parents that *values their status*. This is the best way to compensate for the often tension-filled parent/child relationship. Honor serves as a strong and unbreakable chain, keeping parents and children closely connected.

TEN

The guideline does not have any qualifying statements. There are no stipulations about earning or warranting admiration. Everyone is simply instructed to honor.

Honor appreciates what parents give and does not expect anything in return. Honor does not resent what they are not or what they did not do. Honor is demonstrated through kindness and thoughtfulness. Honor is seen when refraining from behavior diminishing the parent's role. Honor keeps mom and dad connected to the family.

The focus is not just on good parenting skills. Even poor parenting requires honor, if not for the parent than for the child. Many good people go through terrible feelings of regret after a parent dies for failing to honor a cruel mother or father while they were alive.

No exceptions

There was a man, when younger, who was musically and artistically talented. He also had a natural ability with horses, lots of *horse sense*.

As a young husband and father, he was often thoughtful and caring but sadly idolized intoxicating beverages. When drunk he became angry and mean, often abusive to his wife and family. His wife eventually secured a divorce and gained custody of the children.

A daughter weathered the turbulence, got married and had children of her own. Although often challenging, she stayed connected with her dad. He continued making several poor decisions, occasionally homeless and often associating with unsavory characters.

When he became extremely ill, he would be admitted to a State-sponsored care facility. The daughter would be informed of his whereabouts and took time, sometimes traveling long distances, to see him. She brought a new shirt or some underclothes and did what she could to make life more bearable for him.

After his health returned, he would demand an immediate release. The facility had no choice but to let him go. He eventually found his way back to the streets.

In due course, he was placed on disability and rented a room at a poorly maintained motel. The daughter would visit, only after phoning a couple days in advance. If sober the time was extended, if intoxicated the time was shortened. She often brought a favorite hot meal.

TEN

He liked hearing stories about the grandchildren. With a promise to be sober, she would sometimes bring the youngest. Sitting on his lap, her son heard wonderful stories about horses.

The alcohol gradually destroyed the body and took his life. The daughter helped arrange a simple funeral service, saving her money to contribute toward a grave marker.

Did she have a good opinion of him? Partly, yet he did not always behave in a manner warranting admiration.

Did she love him? Yes, at least the kind and caring father she remembered as a little girl, the one telling her wonderful stories about horses, singing country songs, and drawing beautiful pictures.

Did she honor him? Absolutely! She was thoughtful, caring, and kept him connected to the family.

Your future

An old man lived with a son and his family. The meals were eaten together and enjoyable. But his health eventually began to decline, hands started shaking, and food became spilled.

One day, his hand shook so bad the silverware

dropped and broke the plate. Food splattered across the table and onto the carpeting. The son became furious and said, "Dad, I've had enough. You'll have to eat by yourself in your room." He got his father a non-breakable plastic plate and brought him his food each night.

Meals at the dinner table were quieter and neater. Although lonely eating by himself, the man did not want his son upset and said nothing.

The son came home from work one day, right when his teenage daughter was returning from the mall. She purchased a beautiful silver plate, made from scratch-resistant stainless steel. He asked and was told the plate was for him.

Although curious as to why, he decided he would somehow find a good use for it. Yet she said, "It's not for now, but when you are old and your hands shake. Because I love you so much, when you can no longer sit at our table, I want you to have a nice plate for eating in your room." He got the message.

The old man returned that night to the dining table. Meals were noisier and sometimes messy, but the family was whole.

How you treat your parents will impact you.

TEN

Honor

Are you holding anything against a parent or guardian? Let it go! Have you been hurt by mom, dad, or a caregiver? Somewhere along the way, they quit hurting you and you started hurting yourself. Give the pain to Jesus!

Honor helps the home and elevates dignity in society.

SIXTH WORD

ASSASSINATION

"You have heard that it was said to those of old, 'You shall not murder; and whoever murders will be liable to judgment.' But I say to you that everyone who is angry with his brother will be liable to judgment; whoever insults his brother will be liable to the council; and whoever says, 'You fool!' will be liable to the hell of fire. (Matthew 5:21-22)

In the middle of the TEN Words the direction shifts from upward to outward. The first four address connecting with God; the fifth elevates the role parents play in developing sound relations; the last five address associating with one another.

All TEN Words are about relationships. Seeing them as simply *rules for living* takes away their intent. Contentment is associated with how someone builds close and meaningful links with God and those created in his image.

Connecting with God involves entering a covenant, not adulterating oneself with other gods, esteeming him, and giving time weekly to remembering the purpose of life.

Relating to parents involves honoring, more than doting and admiring.

Associating with others involves dignified and non-malicious treatment. Five wrongful actions ruin living with others, listed from the most harmful to the least damaging. All are equally wrong!

The Sixth Word reads, *"You shall not murder."* (Exodus 20:13) Some translations simply record "kill." A more accurate rendering would read *"wrongful* killing."

The worst and most extreme act done to another person is taking their life, ending future opportunities for resolving disputes and reestablishing togetherness. Murder is the most severe abuse against another person.

Taking Life

The first case of murder recorded in Scripture

TEN

happened early after creation. (Genesis 4:1-16) Cain, a son of Adam and Eve, had a problem with what transpired between his brother Abel and the Lord. Sibling rivalry for divine acceptance and association caused Cain to experience anger and agony. He *allowed himself* to consider, agree to, and act upon an evil response.

God attempted to help Cain clarify the issue, but he *opted to* murder rather than pursue a suitable resolve. Failing to regard someone as equally important is the first step towards murder.

Murder is wrong primarily for two reasons: First, it is an attack upon God because all creation is his. Wrongfully taking a life robs the Lord.

People are unique in comparison to all creation. The Lord personally breathed life into the first human, giving a soul and making mankind different. Men and women have both a tangible and intangible element. A spiritual component is deeply rooted in people, making an eternal existence with God possible.

Secondly, murder is linked to what Jesus said in the Sermon on the Mount: "So whatever you wish that others would do to you, do also to them, for this is the Law and the Prophets." (Matthew 7:12) As a matter of social structure, murder is wrong because you do not want to be murdered.

Justifiable killing

Scripture does not condemn all acts of taking life. Some forms of killing are justifiable.

Ending the life of an attacker to protect someone from certain death is not murder. People must come to the aid of those in trouble. Failing to get involved or not wishing to be inconvenienced is wrong, especially in an era of road rage, drive by shootings, violent gangs, and terrorism. No one is allowed to stand back, watch a violent act, and do nothing. A society where no one feels obligated to rescue is one in which no one is ever safe.

Turning the other cheek does not prohibit protecting oneself. When forced to terminate the life of an aggressor, self-defense is not an act of murder.

War and combat are sometimes necessary in an arrogant, greedy, hateful, and abusive world. During the heat of battle, members of the Armed Forces have a duty to uncompromisingly defend and aggressively attack enemies.

Unjustified killing

Other acts of killing are not justified. The human body is not the exclusive property of an individual.

TEN

The vessel of clay is leased and must be returned to the Potter with only reasonable wear and decay.

Intentionally putting yourself in life-threatening situations without just and moral reasons are not permissible. This includes suicide, an act of premeditated killing.

Chemical abuse, whether with a prescription, over-the-counter, or illegal drug, is potentially lethal and wrong.

Promiscuous sex and exposure to numerous life-ending diseases associated with harmful sexual activity are not condoned.

A soul has been divinely placed within an earthen vessel needing mental, emotional, physical, and spiritual care. Taking actions that could terminate the *lease* prematurely is condemned.

Abortion and Euthanasia

Abortion is murder. Many experts attempt to give biological and legal definitions to the beginning of life. Science and legislation will never solve this philosophical and theological debate. Abortion is not about the safety of a mother, which is nothing more than social trickery, a carefully played chess piece on the game board of *selfish* rights. The procedure is often a means of birth control or a convenience from an unwanted pregnancy. The issue is ultimately about pride and arrogance.

Euthanasia is murder, sometimes referred to as mercy killing. The action is sometimes done to relieve families of the difficulties associated with prolonged deaths, more than to mercifully end suffering. The strength of divine grace is available for everyone while a body is experiencing limitations and wasting away.

Capital Punishment

Some equate capital punishment as a murderous procedure. Taking the life of an innocent person is different than a society determining the elimination of an evildoer is the correct response for a criminal act. The death penalty is associated with destroying willful wickedness from among his creation and is a valid form of retribution and deterrence.

State executions should never be deemed necessary strictly by circumstantial evidence, but only after a thorough investigation ends with clear, certifiable, and convincing proof. The application must be done with caution. Unlike murder, *accidental* and *unintentional* taking of life should not be punishable by death.

TEN

Another form of *taking life*

The Sixth Word first appears to have little relevance to the average man or woman. How many plots someone's demise? Very few! Yet people may be closer to violating this directive than often thought.

The Sermon on the Mount gives greater clarity to the issue. Jesus said murder includes *character assassination*, using the mouth as a lethal weapon.

Danger is associated with words. Like a razor-sharp scalpel, the tongue has the power to hurt or heal, depending on use. Every time someone tells misleading stories, they send toxic words that destroy people who have done nothing wrong or harmful.

Reputation is a precious possession. Everyone strives to attain a good name. When predisposed to view someone negatively, the impression affects behavior towards them. When someone loses a good reputation, the future often becomes mortally wounded.

To act angrily toward another and humiliate them is akin to manslaughter. Misrepresenting or intentionally slandering someone can cause them to fail. Killing a career and taking away employment is comparable to homicide. Defamation of character assassinates *livelihood.*

Gossip occurs for mainly three reasons: shaming someone to appear more important; lowering the standings of someone considered more prominent; and, embarrassing someone for entertainment purposes. Children quickly learn the practice, teenagers refine the process, and adults master the performance.

Gossipers sometimes attempt to pass the responsibility to the listener. They begin a scandalous piece of news by saying something like, "This may be gossip but...." Disclaimers are an attempt to transfer responsibility from the *teller* to the *snoop*. No matter the efforts made to justify, nothing changes the fact that character assassination is taking place and murder is occurring.

How to deal with rumors

First, *simply state firsthand information.* The Apostle John began a letter to churches by writing, "That which was from the beginning, which *we* have *heard*, which *we* have *seen* with *our* eyes, which *we* looked upon and have *touched* with *our* hands, concerning the word of life—the life was made manifest, and *we* have seen it, and testify to it and proclaim to you the eternal life, which was with the

Father and was made manifest to us—that which *we* have *seen* and *heard we proclaim* also to you, so that you too may have fellowship with us; and indeed our fellowship is with the Father and with his Son Jesus Christ." (1 John 1:1-3) A genuine witness speaks accurately about their experiences and avoids hearsay.

Should a character issue need attention, the information must be reported factually and only to those responsible for addressing improper conduct. Informing appropriate authorities of anything jeopardizing honesty and integrity is a duty.

Secondly, if someone starts by saying, *"Did you hear the latest rumor about…"* stop them immediately and respond, *"I don't want to hear it!"* Although my mother quit church involvement, she continued having high behavioral standards. I witnessed her use this reply on more than one occasion and saw its effectiveness.

Usually, a gossiper becomes uncomfortable and refrains from future attempts. They may become irritated or insulted; that is their problem. The transfer of responsibility from teller to listener makes a person culpable.

Thirdly, *speaking about someone to someone else gets back to them—guaranteed.* Most everyone becomes the brunt of untrue and unkind comments. The statement and the source eventually get back to the victim, often sooner than a slanderer realizes. Some sufferers of this crime have disciplined themselves to overlook such things, but most people cannot. Relationships easily become strained.

Fourthly, *give the talebearer the benefit of doubt.* Instead of thinking someone was being malicious toward you, assume they did something unwittingly or ignorantly. Friends deserve better than for you to believe the worse of them. Assume the best until clear evidence surfaces of an intentional act.

Gossip and the church

Nothing destroys ministry and kills congregations faster than spreading rumors. The act of gossiping kills the life right out of the church, the *body* of Christ. What becomes annihilated by lethal slander requires a spiritual renewal—*revival* means restoring life.

Jim Cymbala, shortly after arriving at Brooklyn Tabernacle, quickly recognized gossip was killing the congregation. He confronted the problem and people took greater accountability for their comments. The same issue is proving to be a chronic problem in churches throughout the world. Murder may be occurring more under *church steeples* than on *city streets*. The addiction to assassinate character must be aggressively handled.

What about you?

This picturesque bit of prose clearly sums up the issue: (Author unknown)

My name is Gossip. I have no respect for justice.
I maim without killing. I break hearts and ruin lives.
I am cunning and malicious and gather strength with age.
The more I am quoted the more I am believed.
I flourish at every level of society.

My victims are helpless.
They cannot protect themselves against me,
Because I have no face.
To track me down is impossible.
The harder you try, the more elusive I become.
I am nobody's friend.

Once I tarnish a reputation, it is never the same.
I topple governments, wreck marriages, and ruin careers;
Cause sleepless nights, heartaches, and indigestion.
I spawn suspicion and generate grief.
I make innocent people cry in their pillows.

Even my name hisses...gossip.
I make headlines and headaches...

The next comment may appear extremely direct, yet blunt-talking people usually comprehend only frank remarks.

Before you repeat a story ask yourself
is it true, is it fair, is it necessary?
If not...SHUT UP!

If you have a problem with someone, go to them or an appropriate party and seek a resolve. Avoid gossip, the *taking of life*.

The easiest way to stop fatally destroying people is to end the habit of gossiping.

SEVENTH WORD

BETRAYAL

"You have heard that it was said, 'You shall not commit adultery.' But I say to you that everyone who looks at a woman with lustful intent has already committed adultery with her in his heart." (Matthew 5:27-28)

The Assemblies of God church in Marshall, Minnesota, began in 1939. Two sisters by the name of Ruth and Pearl went to Lake Geneva Bible Camp and were deeply impacted by a guest speaker. They invited the minister to come to Marshall and conduct an evangelistic crusade. A tent was placed on the corner of Main and College Street. A new church started a week later.

My wife and I, along with three of our children,

came to oversee the church in 1979. We celebrated the fortieth church anniversary with the congregation and experienced five faith-growing years. Ruth and Pearl, who never married, continued to be actively involved.

The town is known nationally as the recognized headquarters of a couple major industries and the location of Southwest State University. But the place is known by local residents for lousy water.

Two naturally blond teenagers came to church one Sunday with their hair having a reddish tint. I asked in casual conversation if they had highlighted their hair color. They replied that the water softener at their home broke and shampooing in untreated water caused the red results.

Drinking the stuff could cause occasional cramps. It took about six months for my stomach to adjust to living there. My wife developed a digestive ailment she continues dealing with today.

Each summer, I devoted a week at Lake Geneva to help at a Kids or Teen Bible Camp. In 1981, a phone call came from home. This was very unusual; my wife was sensitive about the busyness during camps.

She said she was not feeling well and growing

TEN

increasingly concerned. Then she said, "I think I'm pregnant!"

I *assured* her, she was not expecting. "You're just having another reaction to the water," I said. As a precaution, we determined an appointment with a doctor was in order.

She went to the doctor's office the following week while I stayed home with the kids. When she returned, I asked about the prognosis. She affirmed the water was continuing to cause issues.

Then I asked, "And?"

She said, "I am!"

I asked cautiously, "You are what?"

She said, "I'm pregnant!"

I cried! She put her arms around me and allowed me to literally weep on her shoulder.

I was not opposed to more children in the home. The issue was we were poor. We were more than poor, we were a dictionary definition of poverty, an American poster-child of abject poverty. There was no medical insurance and we just gave away baby furniture to friends attending Bible College in Minneapolis.

People have since asked, "How many children did you want?" Our reply has been, "The ones we have!" All four of the children are very much loved and *wanted*. Not every child was *planned*.

After getting over the surprise, we made the necessary preparations, which included telling the congregation about a new addition to the family. The next Sunday, I thanked everyone for regularly praying about the extreme problem my wife was having with the drinking water. Heads were nodding up and down, affirming and understanding her experiences. I then explained she recently went to a doctor and part of the problem would be resolved in about "nine months."

The church had several younger families. Immediately, the newer moms caught the meaning and their faces lit up with excitement. I happened to look toward Ruth and Pearl, the elderly spinster sisters—their faces were completely blank. After a few moments, they gave a *surprised* look, like the rest of the people.

Initially, I thought they were expressing joy for our personal contribution to church growth. I later found out I misinterpreted their facial appearance. Instead of surprise, they were *shocked*. They could not believe their pastor and lovely pastor's wife did, and I quote, "That!" How did they think we got the other three children?

As a side note, our fourth child has a natural reddish tint to his hair. Fortunately, my dad also had slight red tones to his hair or we might have believed it was caused by the water.

The seventh commandment involves the subject of "that" and needs major attention, especially in this day and age: *"You shall not commit adultery."* (Exodus 20:14) Sexual infidelity is the second worst offense against a person, the second hardest action to reconcile between two people.

Pleasure

The Lord passionately created heaven and earth. On the sixth day, as the final act of creating, he made a man and a *wo*man (*womb*-man, the man species with a womb). They were also called male and *fe*male (*fetus*-male, the male person able to incubate a fetus). They were created *equal*, similarly named and uniformly referred to as *mankind*, but were designed to function differently. He instructed them to come together, procreate, and produce others just like them—people in the image and likeness of God.

At the end of the sixth day and before the seventh day, God gazed upon the completed creation. While admiring the beauty and grandeur of the finished work, his thoughts and feelings were recorded in scripture as, "Very good!" That is putting it mildly! This was a *wow moment*; he was thrilled beyond measure and communicated feelings of ecstasy.

The seventh day of creation was made holy. Among other things, he sanctified *expressions and emotions of creating*. After the first couple rebelled, creation and creating became tainted. Thoughts, feelings, and actions were immediately naked and unseemly, eventually becoming heartless and inappropriate. A beautiful masterpiece became marred.

Wonderful emotions are associated with creating. Exhilaration is more a part of creating than the finished creation, providing the drive and ambition to keep producing. Activities associated with creating cause *wow* moments.

Those involved in the performing arts become easily enraptured by creating, whether in art, music, or drama. Talk to athletes about the emotional high associated with creatively playing an intense game. Similarly, breathtaking feelings of creating are a part of the sexual pleasure.

TEN

Marriage

Not only is he the Creation God but also the Covenant Lord. Made in his image, people have a natural propensity to create *and* naturally crave to abide in covenants, where intimacy dwells. Intimacy and associated feelings are designed to be experienced exclusively under a mutually binding agreement.

Eternal life involves Christ-followers abiding in an everlasting covenant, experiencing lofty feelings of joy, peace, and love. Earthly living involves couples abiding in marriage agreements "'til death do us part," experiencing elevated heights of fulfillment and satisfaction.

Holy union

Two aspects are divinely associated with feelings of intimate sexual pleasure:

First, sexual activity must be able to create. The sexual experience is fulfilling God's plan if two consenting adults have the physical means to join together in a life-creating union.

In making artworks, masterpieces are not always produced yet wonderful feelings are attached to the attempts. In sporting events, no matter the emotional intensity of the game, athletes do not always win. The act of sex is designed as a pleasurable experience for a man and a woman, able to produce life even though life may not result in the act.

Secondly, the sexual activity must be under a covenant. More than companionship, the primary purpose of marriage is procreating.

Some wish to broaden the spectrum of marriage in an effort to achieve an *illusion* of equality and gain a *semblance* of benefits. Yet parity was designed into *creation*, not established by or incorporated into a legal document. Covenant benefits have limitations and stipulations.

Sexual intercourse occurring between a human and animal will not create and cannot happen under a mutually binding covenant. Sexual activity between people with similar sex organs does not create even though a mutually binding agreement can possibly be established. Neither scenario fulfills the intent, purpose, and conditions for sanctioned sexual pleasure.

If a sexual union is not an organic union able to procreate under normal and healthy circumstances *and* is also not done under binding vows, pleasures associated with the activity are not covered by the sanctifying blessing of God and are rendered *unholy*.

TEN

Holy and unholy sex

A world in rebellion is a mixture of holy and unholy. Sexual activity was initially blessed on the seventh day of creation and declared holy. People can defiantly make the divinely created experience otherwise. Out of disobedience they can choose unholy sex.

The sexual activity of a man and a woman in the bonds of marriage is divinely blessed. Marriage is officially referred to as *holy* matrimony. Pleasures associated with sex are designed as a fulfilling expression of intimacy under revered and saintly vows that express undeniable devotion. Every other demonstration of sex is unholy.

Many forms of behavior have been deemed unseemly throughout history. Incest destroys relationships between an adult and adolescent, a parent and offspring, between siblings, extended family, or in-law relatives.

Damaging activity is also related to sexual obsessions void of pure love and minus a physical relationship with another person, including cybersex, sexting, and sexual fantasies.

Non-marital sex (without plans of marriage), premarital sex (before marriage), and extramarital sex (during marriage) are unholy.

Other creatures instinctively engage in sex, reproducing their own kind. Similarly, people involved in sexual impropriety are simply acting like animals.

Jesus clarified the issue in the Sermon on the Mount: inappropriate sexual behavior involves the continual lustful desire for another person, not simply a passing glance or rejected temptation. Problems occur when *continually* looking and allowing the mind to *dwell* on someone without *honorable* intentions. The story of Amnon and Tamar shows the tragic outcome of such behavior. (2 Samuel 13:1-19)

Infidelity

The *second* and *seventh* directives address unfaithfulness—one against God and the other against a person made in his image. The Old Testament book of Malachi refers to betrayal as "breaking faith." *Idolatry* is breaking faith with God and *adultery* is breaking faith with a person.

Statistics about the percentage of people committing adultery are unreliable because people are dishonest about the subject. What has been documented is that infidelity is a major cause of

TEN

divorce. Sadly, the frequency of unfaithfulness is also high within faith communities, dedicated to God.

Society generally and constantly redefines morality in lenient, tolerant, laissez-faire, hands-off, and accommodating ways. Many cultures glamorize, defend, and even promote adultery. Women magazines often place a seal of approval on such behavior, calling it healthy.

One publication suggested affairs can be sexually revitalizing, an escape from a used-up marriage. Another thought a relationship improves by a spouse getting their moment of ecstasy elsewhere, causing less criticism and complaining about their mate. The opposite is what occurs—greater annoyance and more irritation with the spouse.

There is a clear unwillingness to condemn destructive sex. Many avoid making any comments about sexual conduct out of fear of receiving untrue accusations. Who wants to be errantly branded with scornful terms, such as the ever so popular *homophobic*? People can be genuinely and regularly cared for without approving deviate tendencies or condoning errant behavior.

Why unholy sex is harmful

After Adam and Eve rebelled against God, they became embarrassed of nakedness. The covering of marriage reinstates the original freedom. Marriage is beautiful because it covers shame and reveals unrestrained intimacy. A Christ-centered marriage teaches truths about an eternal relationship with the Lord.

Marriage is a state of knowledge. In Scripture, whenever a man had sexual intercourse with a woman, he "*knew*" her and she conceived a child. A person disrobes to another and they gain a new *knowledge* of someone while allowing someone to know them *fully*. They become exposed to another person and begin the quest for a totally uninhibited relationship.

The beauty of eternity involves being fully known and not having further need of marriage. There will be nothing to hide in the presence of the Lord—no guilt or shame. (1 Corinthians 13:12)

If marriage is more than sex but, rather, a lifetime of two people knowing each other, what happens in adultery? Intimacy is violated by disrobing to someone else. The privacy of their relationship is destroyed. Trust is shattered and the quest for relational and spiritual growth becomes

TEN

hindered.

In the older covenant, God called Israel to shame for spiritual adultery. He was outraged at their affection for an idol, even worse, forsaking intimacy with him. Similarly, sexual adultery desecrates marital relations and does not create closeness.

Something beautiful occurs when, in the spirit of grace, two people find forgiveness and acceptance. Unfortunately, skepticism and distrust often prevail even when forgiveness is expressed. Trust, once freely given, must now be earned.

Several advocate adultery and fornication as additional forms of intimacy. On the contrary, they violate intimacy and are simply acts of destructive pleasure. A genuinely intimate relationship means only those within a mutually binding agreement know each other fully.

Human intimacy is designed to help people better understand the depth of intimacy God desires to have with everyone placing faith in him, with those not *breaking faith*.

Run!

The book of Proverbs is full of counsel about damaging sex. A condensed version would read,

"When sexually tempted, run! Do not look back, just run!" A person cannot tame this passionate drive for pleasure. Trying is futile.

While providing leadership at a Bible college, students were regularly instructed by the Dean of Students, "In moments of romantic embrace, a war develops between your will and your passion, between 'I won't do it' and 'my pants are on fire.' When this occurs, passion normally wins."

The easiest way to avoid sexual indiscretions is by not putting yourself in situations leading to sexual fantasies.

Some healthy taboos include no private lunches, no intimate phone calls, no private interludes using electronic media, no personal gifts, and no conversation on marital problems with anyone where a sexual attraction exists.

Stupid explanations

Comments are frequently given to rationalize and validate immoral activity in hopes of making it acceptable:

"I love my family and do not want to leave them. It is better to be unfaithful for the sake of keeping the home intact."

TEN

"My spouse no longer satisfies me sexually and I must find it elsewhere instead of going through an unwanted divorce."

"I live under constant stress, needing frequent relief."

"My lover better understands me."

"My preferences in sexual activity are different than my spouse."

"I have finally found real love."

"My spouse was unfaithful, and I want to settle the score."

"I found my soul mate."

Is there ever a place in a love-covenant for doubt or anxiety to exist with regards to spousal devotion and commitment? No!

What is generally not told about what happens after adultery? Most of those breaking up a marriage to marry someone else are later sorry; many marrying their lover get another divorce; and a good number of those staying married to their lover are not happy.

Success

A longtime friend instructed future ministers to write this formula in the leaf of their Bible: LG + LP + HS + PT = SM.

The meaning? <u>L</u>ove <u>G</u>od; <u>L</u>ove <u>P</u>eople; <u>H</u>ead on <u>S</u>traight; *<u>P</u>ants on <u>T</u>ight*, produces <u>S</u>uccessful <u>M</u>inistry.

Quick review

The TEN Words address relationships with God, parents, and others.

With God, you are to enter into an exclusive covenant, esteeming his good name, and investing personal time.

Connections with mom and dad are preserved by giving them honor.

The worst wrongful act to someone is murder, ending any possibility of mutual understanding. Murder is *wrongful* killing. Yet, *taking life* can be more than *physical death*; it can also be *character assassination*.

Gossip violates the sixth guideline. Have you willfully told an inaccurate or distorted story about someone to someone else, taking away their *livelihood*? Have you allowed yourself to listen to a spiteful story about another person? If so, you either committed murder or was a co-conspirator.

Intimacy

The Ten Commandments was the topic one Sunday in Kids Church. A little boy asked his father afterward, "Daddy, what does it mean when it says, 'Thou shalt not commit *agriculture*?'" With hardly a pause the father replied, "Son, it just means you're not supposed to plow another man's field."

Well said! Stay away from someone else's field. Keep intimacy sacred and holy.

EIGHTH WORD

PILFERING

Let the thief no longer steal, but rather let him labor, doing honest work with his own hands, so that he may have something to share with anyone in need. (Ephesians 4:28)

The First Word calls people to a special association with the Lord, stating, "I am the Lord *your* God." More than just the Creator, he is to become "our Father" (Matthew 6:9)—a personal connection.

The Second addresses loyalty, not committing idolatry against God. A major idol is the selfish trilogy of me, myself, and I.

The Third admonishes esteem for God. His name should not be linked to vain actions, selfish ambitions, or inappropriate activities.

The Fourth gives attention to remembering. Everyone is to regularly recall they have been allotted a certain amount of time and need to fulfill the purpose behind it—worshiping God.

The Fifth gives recognition to the first known authority figure. Parents are the gateway to understanding relations, both with God and those created in his image. Some moms and dads show desirable conduct and others teach detrimental traits. Whether taught positively or negatively (what should be performed, or what should be shunned) they are given honor for their role in life.

The Sixth starts the section addressing relationships with one another. The worst crime against someone is murder, ending any hope of resolving the disagreement. Intentionally taking life includes destroying livelihood.

The Seventh is the second reference to *breaking faith*—disloyalty to a spouse. Infidelity is the second worst wrongful act done to someone, the second hardest offense to resolve. Betrayal is presently promoted as an expression of intimacy. On the contrary, unfaithfulness violates closeness.

The Eighth is the third worst offense causing

damage to relationships: *"You shall not steal."* (Exodus 20:15)

Thievery

Mark Twain during a reflective moment wrote, "When I was a boy, I was walking along a street and happened to spy a cart full of watermelons. I was fond of watermelons, so I sneaked quietly up to the cart and snitched one. Then I ran into a nearby alley and sank my teeth into the melon. No sooner had I done so, however, then a strange feeling came over me. Without a moment's hesitation, I made my decision. I walked back to the cart, replaced the melon, and took a ripe one."

Paul makes a straightforward comment to the church in Ephesus: he directs them to "stop stealing!" (Ephesians 4:28) Pilfering was a way of life in the town and practiced by some following Jesus. They were given the antidote to seek gainful employment and include in their budget a line-item for needy people.

The problem of stealing still influences church-attending people. If a person plans to eventually return it, can something be *borrow*ed indefinitely? Does stealing from a corporation rather than a person make a difference? Is it wrong if the item will not be missed? Is it stealing if a person does not have what others have?

The issue

Stealing goes to the very core of stewardship. The earth and everything in it belongs to the Lord. (Psalms 24:1) Everyone has been given a trust, an obligation to watch over a portion of his property—no more, no less. A parable of Jesus describes different consignment amounts: one, two and five. (Matthew 25:14-18) People have different levels of responsibility for overseeing his possessions and resources.

The entrusted items become an extension of a person's life, as much as their own body. When property becomes stolen, a part of them is taken, part of their stewardship.

When people's homes are burglarized, they often talk of feeling violated, knowing robbers rummaged through intimate belongings looking for valuables. They are repulsed thinking a stranger gained knowledge of personal aspects of their life.

A newspaper reported some thieves robbing two stores in Chicago and forcing everyone to take off their clothes, tangibly demonstrating what happens when things are stolen. A person is stripped of self-worth and left feeling vulnerable.

TEN

Society's approach for dealing with thieves is showing poor results. Jails are full of robbers. Is this an actual deterrent? Incarceration usually makes better crooks of thieves.

Scripture gives a different corrective measure. Thieves need to provide for themselves and repay their victims—give restitution plus a preventive penalty. The older covenant required a twenty percent surcharge for taking property that infringed upon someone's stewardship. Why should a crook end up burdening society?

Explanations

People naturally downplay the seriousness of what is happening, trying to pretend poor actions are justified. They look for ways to make bad conduct appear reasonable, if not allowable. The following sixteen comments are commonly used to support underhanded behavior:

"Wow, look what I found." While leaving a hardware store, I noticed a wallet lying in the parking lot. The billfold was literally bulging with cash and credit cards. "What wonderful luck: 'finders keepers, loser's weepers!'" Wrong! Just because something is found, the property does not transfer to the finder. Whose name is on the credit cards and whose wallet contains the money?

"Their mistake and not my fault." Keeping extra change incorrectly given by a cashier is stealing. Not paying for something mistakenly omitted from a bill is dishonest.

"I deserve it." Some think errors in their favor are designed to even out all the other times they felt short-changed.

"It's only fair considering my situation." An armored car had a collision in an impoverished neighborhood. The back door was jarred opened and a bag of money fell onto the street. Underprivileged adults and children ran everywhere picking up wades of cash. When police arrived, the money was missing. During the investigation, several people considered it divine intervention, an act of God. The Lord does not want recognition for the lack of integrity. The haves and have-nots are under the same moral obligation not to steal.

"I couldn't help myself." A church treasurer misused a large amount of church funds over several years. When confronted, the person complained of experiencing frequent and high levels of anxiety and stress. Take a long run or a warm bath instead.

"It's not hurting anyone." This is frequently done to support bogus insurance claims, phony malpractice suits, and spurious litigations. Many are

convinced only corporations, not individuals, are being financially impacted. The loss may even appear minimal on the ledger of a multimillion-dollar business. Yet, rates are increased to cover phony claims, which steals from the insured. Prices are inflated to cover the cost of shoplifting, which steals from the customers. Believing no one is getting hurt causes higher premiums and prices—everyone pays.

"I work here and earned it." Embezzling, taking office supplies, and doing personal business on company time is stealing.

"I'll pay when I can." Failing to compensate employees on payday and failing to timely pay a submitted bill after a completed job is stealing.

"I was only borrowing it." This is learned early in life by siblings using a sister's sweater or a brother's jacket. Borrowing means asking permission beforehand. Until the owner is notified an item is stolen.

"The fool deserves it." Commonly used by someone angrily taking items as an act of revenge.

Falsifying information on tax forms is stealing. "But politicians stupidly use my hard-earned tax dollars." If you do not like government waste, vote for new leadership and for better accountability.

"I didn't take anything tangible." Stealing occurs when lying about your age for a cheaper entrance charge, reduced meal price, or a courtesy discount. An object may not have been taken but *profit* was stolen.

Some students cheat on exams. Cheating steals a grade. If you cheat on exams, please do not design the plane I travel in or perform surgery on my family. You probably do not know your job well enough.

"Nothing personal, just business." False and misleading advertising is wrong. People feel cheated and do take it personally.

A woman bought a lamp on sale at a chain store and went to a different outlet for a full refund. While standing in a check-out line, she bragged to a friend about gaining a twenty percent profit. This is stealing!

"I didn't know I bought a stolen piece of merchandise." Something brand new sold in a back alley is probably *hot* and not a legitimate *close out* sale. Buying stolen property makes a person an accomplice.

"It's not much." Size or amount is not the issue. If it was not bought, earned, inherited, or received as a gift, it belongs to someone else.

TEN

"I did it for a good cause." People sometimes attempt to smuggle or sneak items, considered illegal by a foreign government, into the country. A right cause never justifies a wrong means. Both the process and results must be honorable.

Finally, the granddaddy of them all, *"Everyone else is doing it."* This is often said by rioters breaking in and stealing from stores. Local merchants, well known and respected members of the community, witness neighbors behaving like thieves.

Children are tragically robbed of innocence; ideas are stolen from inventors; stealing is growing exponentially on the World Wide Web. The problem is virtually endless.

Here is a rather bizarre excuse: A young man was arrested for stealing a car. He stated he found the automobile in front of a cemetery and thought the owner was dead. Dumb!

Vulnerable

In everyone's life, some things tempt more than others and some issues are easier to overcome. While talking to younger ministers about integrity, I warn against *gold, glory, and Gloria* (riches, fame, and intimacy). Usually, a person has a weakness in only one area; rarely does someone struggle in all three.

Know where you are most vulnerable and keep up your guard.

Some chase after wealth and luxury. The problem is not reserved only for the rich. Many without financial means think and talk about nothing else. This passion attacks the poor as well as affluent.

Some seek fame and notoriety. Craving personal attention and wishing admiration causes damage in every profession.

Some pursue secret encounters where moments of pleasure and fantasy become fulfilled. What is done in secret eventually becomes disclosed.

What is your weakness? Which guidelines are more challenging to obey? Where are extra precautionary measures needed?

Raised in an unchurched home and placing faith in God as an older teenager, overcoming stealing was intensely difficult. I was a masterful shoplifter, a highly successful thief—never caught. Stealing was done for momentary thrills, the greater the challenge the bigger the temptation. I rarely needed the stolen items and often threw them away.

When I decided to follow Jesus, stealing was one of three areas causing immediate conviction;

vulgarity and lying were the other two. Taking something not belonging to me had to end.

The precautions I presently take often appear extreme, yet friends and associates cannot imagine the magnitude of control stealing had over me.

Sanctified possessions

Annually, many churches in America promote "Sanctity of Human Life Sunday." There is also the sanctity of property—possessions are an extension of a person, entrusted to them by God.

Unfortunately, stealing is a major problem infiltrating every faith community. The warning to early church believers needs to be applied just as much today: Stop stealing!

NINTH WORD

FALSEHOOD

Now the chief priests and the whole council were seeking false testimony against Jesus that they might put him to death, but they found none, though many false witnesses came forward. (Matthew 26:59-60)

And they stirred up the people and the elders and the scribes, and they came upon [Stephen] and seized him and brought him before the council, and they set up false witnesses who said, "This man never ceases to speak words against this holy place and the law." (Acts 6:12-13)

Do not lie to one another, seeing that you have put off the old self with its practices and have put on the new self, which is being renewed in knowledge after the image of its creator. (Colossians 3:9-10)

The Ninth Word reads, *"You shall not give false testimony against your neighbor."* (Exodus 20:16)

Both Matthew and Acts reveals a sad truth: falsely testifying links a person with the crucifixion of Jesus and the execution of Stephen (the first church martyr).

The second to the last ethical boundaries is three-dimensional: perjury, lying, and hypocrisy.

Perjury

Perjury is *lying under oath*, a legal matter. God is about justice. Truth is a prerequisite to correct rulings. Only when there is an accurate portrayal of what actually happened can fairness be properly administered. Perjury creates injustice.

During a brief period of insanity, I took a few moments to view a telecast of a small-claims court, aired daily. I stopped watching before the program was over. A judge sat behind the bench trying to determine which, the plaintiff or defendant, was lying the *least*. For the excitement of being seen on television and gaining a small amount of money, perjury is regularly committed before a viewing audience.

People commonly lie in a court of law, yet upon

TEN

taking a witness stand the testifier agrees to tell the "truth...so help me God." How can anyone take an oath to speak truthfully only to give a false testimony? Due to a lack of obvious and immediate heavenly intervention, people imagine they are getting away with deception.

If someone is a good enough talebearer, they can deceitfully win the argument; that is, until they stand in the Heavenly Court of Final Retribution. One day, everyone will appear before the Supreme Judge who is never deceived. Presently, the scales of justice frequently seem imbalanced, but he sees and will administer justice.

The patriarch Abraham said it best when presenting his case to spare Sodom and Gomorrah from the consequences of their wicked behavior: "Shall not the Judge of the whole earth do right?" Yes!

Problems with the legal system are supposedly judges being soft on crime, jurists failing to address the rights of victims, and adjudicators rendering racially-biased verdicts. Although valid concerns, corruption is a greater deficiency. When witnesses lie in court, the results are filled with flaws. Deceptive distortions make true justice unobtainable.

Occasionally, testimonies are an erroneous

observation. Most of the time, however, lying is either payback or an attempt to achieve a favorable decision.

A major obstacle to social freedom is a sleazy court system. Judicial proceedings are only as good as the morals of those being served. To live in liberty, justice must be based on *honesty*.

Lies

The cover of a leading news magazine once read, "Lying is in." A book entitled The Day America Told the Truth reveals the nation is consumed with lying. The deficiency has clearly gone worldwide.

One study reveals less than ten percent of Americans regularly tell the truth and a high number are not able to get through a single day without deliberate acts of deceit. People, in general, have gradually drifted away from being honest and truthful.

Falsehood is readily accepted. Words such as *embellished truth* or *white lie* are often used to soften the blow of what is occurring—a blatant disregard for honesty and a deliberate decision to deceive. If it serves their purpose, many who regularly address the general public or speak in open forums will easily

TEN

and effortlessly lie.

People lie to gain attention, to protect themselves from deserved consequences, to cover up guilt, for revenge, and for convenience. Lying, however, is part of a larger trend, serving *individuality*. Falsehood is considered good and acceptable if done to appease personal wants.

Delusion serves friendly enterprise. The fabricated claims of advertisers are part of being competitive.

Deceitfulness serves free speech. Cases are on court dockets because someone thinks expressing exaggerations is the right of open communication.

Dishonesty serves frivolous entertainment. The internet considers a person responsible for figuring out misrepresentations and to not accept everything at face value.

Duplicity, however, makes certain things impossible: there can be no abiding friendships, no honorable business relationships, no fidelity in marriage, and no cohesion in families. All relations require trusting one another, which only comes from truth. Without trust, there is no glue and, ultimately, no confidence in any association.

My children regularly heard me say, "You are not perfect; you will make mistakes. I can handle an error in judgment but will not tolerate lies." The older children often warned the younger siblings, "For heaven sake, no matter what you did, tell Dad the truth. He knows if you lie and the consequences are worse."

Although obligated to tell the truth, no one is required to reveal all their thoughts. Suppose an unattractive woman came to a therapist for marital counseling and qualified her comments by saying, "I know I'm not some raving beauty." At that moment, she is not looking for perfect candor with regards to her less than attractive appearance. Honesty means everything said is true, not everything true should be said.

Silence is not deception; not all truth is worth disclosing. If people seriously wanted absolute frankness, life would be ruder than it already is. There is such a thing as courtesy. People of goodwill watch their words.

Have you ever been asked for an opinion without knowing the thoughts of the person asking? Has someone ever said to you, "What do you think…?" and you quickly comment without any forethought? Not knowing the reason behind a question or failing to understand their point of view creates wedges, even if unintentionally. Why not respond, "Why do you ask?" With a little courtesy, answers can be given without personal insult.

Another growing trend is using flattery in misleading ways. Dishonesty happens when people are led to believe something about themselves that is not true. In an effort to build *self-esteem* parents, teachers, and coaches are causing children and teenagers to believe lies about talents, skills, and abilities. The worst kind of mentor is one that strengthens a false perception.

Be cautious! Avoid giving praise for mediocre efforts or average results. A pat-on-the-back is not sincere if given undeservedly. A compliment is genuine only when warranted. Make praise priceless and precious. Use admiration as a tool for strengthening character and generating effort, rather than for inflating ego.

There is no *right to lie* in the United States Constitution. You can either decline to answer or answer honestly. Truth is a divine quality, strive for it! Followers of Jesus are to manifest "the way, the *truth,* and the life." (John 14:6)

Hypocrisy

Out of the adventures of the Old West comes the

outlaw Jesse James. He killed someone in a bank robbery and shortly thereafter was baptized in the Kearney Baptist Church. He killed another man, a bank cashier, then joined the church choir and taught hymn singing. He liked Sundays but did not always show up at church—on two occasions, he robbed trains instead.

Hypocrisy is acting or speaking in a way to elicit certain *perceptions*, and only for the sake of that perception. Life becomes a stage lived behind a mask. *Hypocrite* is a Greek word describing people that are impure within yet showing outward goodness.

Followers of Jesus are to be a true witness of him, revealing his story to everyone. This includes attitudes, motives, actions, words, practices, beliefs and conduct. Falsely representing him to others is unacceptable. What people desperately need to see is an authentic depiction of Christ in his followers.

Many believers regularly pray the Lord's Prayer. What is being expressed?

"*Our Father in heaven…*" Does your life reflect a holy God as your father?

"*Hallowed be your name…*" Hallowed means honored or revered. Do others see a life reverencing the Lord? Do you esteem him or rather use him for personal gain?

"*Your kingdom come...*" Do your actions demonstrate a desire for righteousness to reign over everything associated with you?

"*Your will be done...*" Is this true? Do you really want God to bring you face-to-face with his will? Do you honestly desire to experience his purpose for your life? Some only prefer an agenda that fits the parameters of their prejudice and goes along with their plans.

Many recite the Lord's Prayer hypocritically. They have developed a kind of *selective vision*, allowing them to be *connected to church* and *carnal in commerce*.

Falsehood

Shortly after committing my life to Christ, both the eighth and ninth commandments were a major cause of conviction. A good thief must be an excellent liar; I was masterful in both areas.

Giving a believable lie is only possible by having a highly-capable mind. A competent liar must be able to keep all the stories straight and show an element of interconnectedness in all the tales. I took a good gift from God, entrusted to my stewardship, and used it in a shameful way.

Addressing falsehood involved learning how to be truthful, which for me was easier said than done. Ways of thinking had to change, dramatically. My mind evaluated every sentence while talking; every word leaving my mouth was scrutinized.

If something was said slightly inaccurate, a silent alarm went off in my head screaming "Untrue!" and I *forced* myself to correct the comment. A lot of correcting was initially required and is still sometimes necessary.

The problem of lying requires a lifetime of vigilance. The reward for truth is being able to look in a mirror and like yourself.

Deception

An outgrowth of having once been an extremely competent liar is an ability to quickly detect lies from others. I may not necessarily confront a liar but my opinion of them becomes deeply influenced. Others have the same capability and respond in similar ways.

For several years I was privileged to serve on a statewide leadership team overseeing churches.

TEN

Occasionally, the Superintendent would ask me to investigate an allegation against a minister. The first appointment was always with the individual in question.

The conversation would start by making sure they were aware of the accusation. The next comment was critical. "You have one opportunity to be completely honest with me. If you have done something wrong and are truthful, we will find a remedy. If you choose to lie, your standings as a minister will be in jeopardy."

During the investigation, after obvious evidence toward their guilt surfaced, watching them continue to use deception was heartbreaking. They were given due notice and ended up needlessly losing ministerial credentials. With truth, there is remedy; with deception, there is shame.

Be real

Honorable ambitions for God and a genuine portrayal of Jesus involves honesty. Lying reveals that someone is *choosing* to join forces with the devil, the father of lies. (John 8:44)

When failing to live godly, pure, honest, and Spirit-filled, the result is a *false witness*. As stated earlier, a false witness automatically is linked with those crucifying Jesus and executing Stephen.

Perjury, lies, and hypocrisy undermines social, marital, and personal relations. Behind murder, adultery, and stealing, falsehood is the fourth worst offense against someone—the fourth hardest action to find a remedy with others.

TENTH WORD

GREED

Finally, brothers, whatever is true, whatever is honorable, whatever is just, whatever is pure, whatever is lovely, whatever is commendable, if there is any excellence, if there is anything worthy of praise, think about these things. (Philippians 4:8)

Each guideline is emphasized by a single word. The TEN Words, as translated in the Jewish Bible, are more than *rules to live by* but are truths for *sincere relationships*. God created social beings. The meaning of life is linked to community. Every personal association has purpose and can bring greater fulfillment to human existence.

The first four words ensure intimate relations with God; the fifth ensures a satisfying connection with family; the last five ensure wholesome involvement with others. Violating these guidelines destroys the foundation of an enjoyable life.

Here is a focused summary of the first nine ethical boundaries: Vertically, have a personal, exclusive, respectful bond with God, weekly remembering the sacred purpose of life. Transversely, honor parents for teaching the value of relationships. Horizontally, physically and verbally protect the life of others, having the highest regard for sexual behavior, honoring the stewardship of personal possessions, while living honestly and speaking authentically.

Self-indulgence

The Tenth Word reads: *"You shall not covet your neighbor's house; you shall not covet your neighbor's wife, or his male servant, or his female servant, or his ox, or his donkey, or anything that is your neighbor's."* (Exodus 20:17)

The leading question generated by this statement is: Are relationships only impacted by what someone *does*? Interactions are also deeply influenced by what is happening *inside*—issues of the heart.

Coveting is a problem in ambitions and aspirations. Wrong actions do not exclusively originate from external conditions. Conduct comes

TEN

from passions and yearnings.

Some mistakenly promote, "Everything's okay as long as it doesn't hurt anyone." Immoral, unkind, and unjust acts do not simply begin with a deed but from a sequence of longings and feelings. Appropriate inward deliberation leads to proper outward behavior.

Coveting becomes confusing because the compelling force of *wanting* is a necessary part of life. Without drive, there is a lack of energy and motivation. Desiring advancement, yearning for improvement, and sharpening skills are healthy aspects of ambition.

Coveting is the force of wanting gone *out of control*. Coveting wishes for *more* than what is right. Coveting is an *unrestrained* impulse to master or possess. Coveting is a world too small in resources to satisfy *infinite* passions.

The Tenth Word addresses wanting something at the expense of someone else, not just wanting. Paul wrote the church in the town of Philippi that combating covetousness involves every thought being refined by divine grace. (Philippians 4:8-9)

Birthing evil actions

A story from the life of Ahab illustrates the intense internal struggle that combats right actions. (1 Kings 21) The king wanted land neighboring his place of residence and asked the owner about purchasing the piece. The proprietor had deep convictions against selling. He felt morally obligated to protect the family heritage. The property had deep sentimental value—priceless. No amount of money could ever be suitable.

The king began brooding over the landowner's unbending decision. His sweet and adorable wife, Jezebel, assured him she would resolve the matter for her big hunk of a man. Shortly afterward, the neighbor was falsely accused of disloyalty and executed. Ahab quickly appropriated the property.

Covetousness caused the violation of three additional wrongs: false witness, murder, and stealing. Three *doing* bans were broken when the *greed* warning was violated. A coveting heart *causes* evil actions.

When someone covets, the act of acquiring takes on a life of its own. The coveting heart wonders, "How much stuff is enough?" and responds, "More than I have!"

TEN

Ask a lottery millionaire a year or two after winning, "Are you any happier today?" A high number, if honest, would have to admit they are not. How many new things can someone buy? How many vehicles can anyone use at any given time and on a regular basis?

For every nice thing, there is always something nicer. The perfect something is yet to be discovered and is always somewhere in the future. Spending your way to happiness is futile.

Additional words associated with coveting are *envy* and *jealousy*. When the focus is more on what a person *does not have* than on *what they have*, problems follow. Possessions begin to rule instead of the person. The question is, who will be *master* and who is the *slave*?

The need to acquire things enslaves and consumes. Only with the ability to firmly control personal wants and wishes is a joyful life discovered.

A culture of greed

The typical consumer is the recipient of thousands of advertisements *daily*. The standard message in commercials is that problems are solved by purchasing products. Many live beyond their means because of believing they need all the goods and conveniences marketed.

Happiness is often portrayed as connected to accruing a lot of things, but people are not any happier owning an abundance of possessions. Stuff without purpose has little reward.

The value of life is derived by counting blessings. Everything someone *has* and *does not have* is a blessing established by heaven. People are to be content and find meaning in whatever circumstances they find themselves.

The Apostle Paul shortly after writing about the importance of correct thinking wrote, "Not that I am speaking of being in need, for I have learned in whatever situation I am to be content. I know how to be brought low, and I know how to abound. In any and every circumstance, I have learned the secret of facing plenty and hunger, abundance and need. I can do all things through him who strengthens me." (Philippians 4:11-13)

Competing

Some individuals are highly competitive; they have to win and are dissatisfied when they come up short. But value is not found in winning but in appreciating the effort to succeed.

TEN

The great football coach Vince Lombardi made famous the line, "Winning is not everything; it is the only thing." Yet, coveting the achievements of someone else downplays individual capabilities and creativity, as well as destroys personal ingenuity and initiative.

There is a myth attached to the idea of contentment: satisfaction is not the lack of drive and motivation but is about *appreciating the moment* in every phase of life. Happiness means being thankful for what you have *and* not consumed by what is absent. Life is filled with grief, disappointment, and pain when contentment is deemed insignificant and discarded.

Fulfillment in life is fully experienced when the blessing associated with each situation is pursued and discovered. Pleasure does not come from corporate titles and wealth, exotic sites and events, accumulated awards and recognition, but by what is done with or without those amenities and pleasantries.

No one appreciates their potential when gratitude is absent, or expectations are idealistic, or conditions are measured by what others experience. Life is cheapened when graded by how someone else lives and only leads to bitterness.

Needs and wants

My youngest son, while in high school, taught me a great lesson. One day, I noticed his dress shoes were very worn and, in comparison to his feet, looked undersized. I asked and was told that not only were they old and worn but two sizes too small. His rationale for not telling me was they were only worn on Sundays. I immediately decided to replace them.

My wife and I did some preliminary scouting. We found a couple of stores with very fashionable shoes at a reduced price. I was searching for shoes thinking as an adult instead of an older teenager.

Picking up our son after school, I said, "We found some great looking shoes on sale for you to look at, a neat pair of wingtips and a couple of attractive slip-ons"—clearly not the taste of most modern-day youth.

After a long spiel about our successful search, I quit talking. From the backseat of the vehicle the silence was broken with these words: "Dad, I'm just a simple man." Many would benefit if they would take a similar approach to life.

A good dose of reality comes by visiting underprivileged nations. Many homes in other cultures have virtually nothing. On a trip to Africa, I

TEN

found myself wondering why anyone should have two of anything when so many do not even have one.

Possessions are a divine gift and not evil, nor are they inconsequential to the Lord. Their value is the ability to enhance and impact the world for his glory. When the accumulation of things becomes the goal and the final objective, the items are idols.

Material motivations are natural and normal. A comfortable home, reliable transportation, and a good income is nothing to feel guilty about, just do not crave what is owned or achieved by someone else.

Jealousy over what another person has is questioning God about his fairness. Have you ever silently and secretively asked yourself, "Why does that person have what I don't?" You are demonstrating a lack of trust in the Lord for what is best for your life. You can ask God to help improve your situation or covet what someone else has, but you cannot do both.

The last few decades have shown an increase in spouses coveting new partners, families coveting excessive possessions, and parents coveting careers over well-rounded children. The destruction of society starts with the heart condition of its citizens.

The end

The Tenth Word is about the internal drives causing external actions. A person can fulfill the first nine and still be filled with envy, jealousy, and greed, resenting what others do or have. Godliness can be sullied by the rotting of the human soul, as well as by human behavior and speech.

The Tenth Word is the exclamation point to the First Word: place your faith in God and trust him with every aspect of life.

FINAL WORD

LOVE

A look at the TEN Words is not complete without seeing the transforming power of the Lord Jesus Christ: The living, beginning and end WORD.

In the beginning was the Word, and the Word was with God, and the Word was God.... In him was life, and the life was the light of men.... But to all who did receive him, who believed in his name, he gave the right to become children of God,... And the Word became flesh and dwelt among us, and we have seen his glory, glory as of the only Son from the Father, full of grace and truth.... For the law was given through Moses; grace and truth came through Jesus Christ. (John 1:1,4,12,14,17)

Jesus said, "Do not think that I have come to abolish the Law or the Prophets; I have not come to abolish them but to fulfill them. (Matthew 5:17)

"Teacher, which is the great commandment in the Law?" And [Jesus] said to him, "You shall love the Lord your God with all your heart and with all your soul and with all your mind. This is the great and first commandment. And a second is like it: You shall love your neighbor as yourself. On these two commandments depend all the Law and the Prophets." (Matthew 22:36-40)

Owe no one anything, except to love each other, for the one who loves another has fulfilled the law. For the commandments, "You shall not commit adultery, You shall not murder, You shall not steal, You shall not covet," and any other commandment, are summed up in this word: "You shall love your neighbor as yourself." Love does no wrong to a neighbor; therefore love is the fulfilling of the law. But put on the Lord Jesus Christ, and make no provision for the flesh, to gratify its desires. (Romans 13:8-10, 14)

For through the law I died to the law, so that I might live to God. I have been crucified with Christ. It is no longer I who live, but Christ who lives in me. And the life I now live in the flesh I live by faith in the Son of God, who loved me and gave himself for me. (Galatians 2:19-20)

Society generally sees the Ten Commandments as *personal restrictions*. Yet, the statements were designed to open the doorway to *significant relationships*.

If people were totally isolated there would be no need for divine guidelines, but everyone is designed to live in community. Everyone is custom made to have relations with the *person* who formed the world, the *parents* bringing them into the world and the *populace* of the world. Ethical conduct is needed to experience thoughtful and caring interaction with others.

The Gospel writers reveal the role of the TEN Words as new covenant believers. There is no contradiction between Jesus' teachings and the directives of the older covenant. His coming did not abolish them but completely and perfectly satisfied them. Instead of negating their authority they take on new dimensions in Christ, summed up in one word: *love*. The proclamations are transformed from *must* to *want*.

Before asking Jesus to reign over my life, the Ten Commandments were stated as rules, both at home and in school. Learning them did not make me want to follow them; I was simply told what was considered right and wrong. But love for God became a force igniting the desire to do everything possible to enhance my association with him and with others, which included abiding by the guidelines of the TEN Words.

With a love for God, everyone can respond to the first four words. *With a love* for one another a person can apply the last six, neighbor implying *anyone* with whom there is contact, including parents.

Judaism teaches 613 commands are in the Law, one for each letter in the Ten Commandments. The rules consist of 248 positive permissions ("you shall") and 365 negative prohibitions ("you shall not"). The positive and negative were also subdivided into major and minor commands, some considered more important and others considered less. Divisions were based on the complexity to obey.

Jesus was asked about the great commandment, in other words, which is the hardest to keep? He responds that two guiding principles cover the intentions of all ten words, and love is the summation of every course of action. Out of love, the statements become life-giving.

Jesus taught and demonstrated that God did not make pronouncements simply to give burdensome demands—they are love-based.

TEN

Loving God

The FIRST Word reveals the personal side of God; "I am the Lord *your* God," a proclamation of a *personal* deity in a *position* of absolute rule. People are to have a covenant connection with him similar to a marriage commitment and a parent/child bond, both involving binding obligations.

An association with God has responsibilities and benefits. "Praise the LORD, O my soul, and forget not all his benefits." (Psalms 103:2) The main advantage is deliverance and liberty from slavery to evil.

Many advocate God's ways are restrictive, but the opposite is true. He sets people free from a world system *falsely* portrayed as a place of fulfillment and satisfaction.

The SECOND Word reveals the exclusive nature of a relationship with the Lord. The goal is negating all the faulty reinforcements that alienate people from the one True God.

People through the ages have wondered what God looks like and have attempted to give Him shape and design. The Lord is not contained in material form or in any aspect of nature. He is greater than the universe, surpassing the limited sensory capabilities.

There are numerous lesser gods. Charming personalities, gifted performers, and talented athletes are especially prominent, but the number one idol is *me, myself, and I*. People think too much of themselves and have become the most sophisticated form of idolatry. Many feelings, desires, looks, and ideas are now idolatrous.

The THIRD Word reveals the importance of *esteem*. The Lord takes issue with how his name is used. An immediate threat of punishment is attached to misuse. Those aligned with God are to uphold his righteous status. Awe for him diminishes when the Lord obtains a bad reputation.

Admiration is critical. Using God's name frivolously displays irreverence; not fulfilling an oath misrepresents him; pretending a special relationship with him for personal gain is shameful; using vulgarity shows arrogance; insincere repentance is worthless.

Holding his name in highest regards shows the sacred nature of associating with God. Actions must never defame him.

The FOURTH Word reveals the importance of remembering. One day each week is solely dedicated to God instead of exclusively devoted to leisure. More than time off from work, the day is for

TEN

remembering the purpose and meaning of life.

Life changes from the mundane to the holy during the Rest Day—a time for finding meaning in the moment. Everyone needs to stand back and view life from an eternal perspective regularly.

Most people are too busy to consider the value of life, ending up frustrated and living with a sense of hopelessness. Every seven days the *why* question is given prayerful consideration, making possible an ability to more effectively deal with the numerous *how* questions surfacing throughout the other six days. The author of time adds significance to human existence when time is put aside for him.

The first four words enhance a *love* encounter with God.

Loving one another

The FIFTH Word affirms the important role of parenting: mom and dad sit at the crossroad of all associations. People understand how to relate to both God and neighbor because of them. As the first authority figure in life, they are given honor.

Nothing is stated about *esteeming* parents. Some lose this because of abusive behavior. Nothing is mentioned about *feeling good* about them. This is often jeopardized whenever appropriate conduct is demanded from a child. Parents are to be treated in a way that reflects their *status* as parents, *appreciating* their efforts and not resenting what they did or did not do.

The SIXTH Word addresses the issue of *wrongful* killing, taking life. Life comes from God and human existence is tied to him. When someone takes a life, they steal from the Lord.

Another form of murder is character *assassination*. Slander, viewing someone negatively, has the power to kill. Gossip destroys a good reputation and impacts *livelihood*.

The SEVENTH Word addresses the betrayal of intimacy. Scripture distinguishes between holy and unholy sex. Holy sex is between a man and a woman in a marital covenant. Unholy sex is every other kind of sexual activity: incest, fornication, adultery, homosexuality, cybersex, sexting, and bestiality.

When someone loves a person, they do not behave in ways that cause their minds and hearts to have pain, fear, doubt or uncertainty.

The EIGHTH Word addresses the issue of property. Possessions are an extension of people. God gives to every person a trust, a level of responsibility for a portion of his world. He entrusts specific items to their stewardship, property becomes attached to them. Stealing takes away part of someone's responsibility to the Lord.

Excuses are often associated with pilfering, deceiving a thief into believing their actions are justified. If not bought, earned, inherited or received as a gift, the item belongs to someone else.

The NINTH Word addresses falsehood. Untrue testimonies associate people with those crucifying Jesus and executing Stephen (the first church martyr). The guideline is a warning against perjury, lying, and hypocrisy.

People lie for revenge, to protect themselves from deserved consequences, to cover up guilt, to gain attention, and for convenience. Deceit and cover-ups make it impossible for abiding friendships, honorable business dealings, trust in marriage, and cohesion in the family. Ambitions must be honest, genuine, and real.

The TENTH Word concerns the heart—a person's thoughts, feelings, and motives. God is concerned with what is happening on the *inside*. Actions stem from the inner nature.

Covetousness devises evil. All other deceptive

actions are an *expression* of evil, but coveting *gives birth to* them. Problems occur when obsessed with the apparent advantage of others, leading to misery, grief, and sometimes depression.

Appreciate your own life. Recognize the blessings of what *you have* and *do not have*. You can believe, ask God for help, and trust him for a better situation, or you can covet—you cannot do both.

The last six words enhance a love encounter with others.

A love-based response to his guidelines

Mother Teresa once said, "Love to be real must cost. It must hurt. It must *empty us of self*." Each of the TEN Words requires giving up selfish actions, words, and thoughts.

The soul has only limited capacity. By emptying wickedness, room becomes available for more righteousness. The response given by Jesus about the great commandment reveals that a sense of worth requires regular and ongoing housecleaning.

Thoughtful and caring associations require regularly putting aside selfishness. Through the Lord Jesus, the *alpha* and the *omega*, the *first* and the *final* WORD (Revelation 22:13), the *ten* ethical boundaries are transformed into *two* life-giving guidelines and provides the best foundation for purposeful, lifelong, and eternal relationships.

Abiding in TWO is much more fulfilling than following TEN.

S. ROBERT MADDOX

ACKNOWLEDGEMENTS

Public servants have a better understanding of law and order. My ministry was deeply influenced by people serving in areas of crime prevention. I was fortunate to become acquainted with gifted people upholding justice. These individuals provided me clear insight and sound reasoning. Their thoughts about impartiality served as priceless treasures, enhancing my values.

South Dakota

Carroll Boze, Doug Noyes, Allen Nelson, and Clayton Pummel

Minnesota

Ken Nordin

Illinois

Rob Campbell, Hal Kaufman, Bob Lowen, and Doug Miller

Missouri

John Ashcroft

Thank you for your dedication to service.

TEN

ABOUT THE AUTHOR

Bob was born and raised in the Pacific Northwest. While serving in the Armed Forces during the Vietnam era, he met his wife, Brenda. They have lived in seven States and raised their four children mostly in the greater Chicago area. They presently reside in southern Missouri.

His career has been as a church overseer, a college administrator, a church denomination leader, a classroom instructor, an athletic coach, and an international emissary.

Bob is an ordained minister, as well as a nationally accredited high school volleyball coach. He is passionate for all generations to enter a life-changing relationship with God and have a fully integrated life through Christ.

He continues to write, teach, and speak in various settings. To view more of his current reflections, his blogs can be found at bob-maddox.blogspot.com. His other ten books are available online.

BOOKS BY THE AUTHOR

SPIRIT Living, *abundantly following Jesus*

GOD, *who are You? Reflections from the names of God in the Bible*

TEN Words, *Reflections from the Ten Commandments*

BLESSING and battles, *Reflections on the Blessing of God and the Battles of Life*

ACTION, *Reflections from the gospel of Mark*

The **CHURCH**, *Reflections from Paul's letter to the Ephesians*

practical **FAITH**, *Reflections from James' letter to the Church*

pure **LOVE**, *Reflections from John's first letter to followers of Jesus*

COMFORT, *Reflections from Paul's second letter to the Corinthians*

really **READY**, *Reflections from the prophetic book of Daniel*

"I Didn't See What Was Coming!", ***LIVING*** *in Christ*

Available in Hardback, Paperback, and eBook editions.

www.ingramcontent.com/pod-product-compliance
Lightning Source LLC
Chambersburg PA
CBHW071507040426
42444CB00008B/1540